VISUAL COMMUNICATION

HOW TO CREATE HIGH-IMPACT NEWSLETTERS

Dozens of right way/wrong way examples to help you create visually powerful newsletters that people will read

■ ■ JANE K. CLELAND

TABLE OF CONTENTS

INTRODUCTION

Everything you need to know to ensure your newsletter's success is explained in this book. Techniques and shortcuts, grounded in research and proven to have worked for others, are detailed so you can adapt these professional strategies easily and quickly. While there is no magic formula, there are many guiding principles that work.

In the pages that follow, these guiding principles are fully explained. You'll see dozens of examples, and read, in easy-to-understand language, the how and why of newsletter editors' decisions. You will be able to approach your newsletter projects with increased confidence.

The examples collected here are from a variety of organizations producing a wide array of newsletters, each targeting different audience types. Because examples of newsletters come from organizations which are both large and small, profit and nonprofit, and these newsletters are used for both internal and external purposes, there are sure to be several examples targeting readers similar to yours. Certain other examples can be easily modified and adapted to suit your newsletter's purpose.

In order to use this book and understand the management, writing, editing, and design principles which are discussed, you need to be familiar with the terminology of the field. The glossary defines key terms and explains how they're generally used by professionals. The first time a word included in the glossary is used, it will appear in boldface. When you see a word in boldface, you can turn to the glossary and familiarize yourself with the term's meaning and conventions.

Both novices and experienced professionals will benefit from this book. For those of you just starting out, this book will help you get on the right track. Those of you with experience will pick up dozens of specialized tips, learn about new trends, and discover desktop publishing shortcuts. Whether your newsletter is tapped out on an old Underwood typewriter and reproduced on a photocopier, or produced using the most sophisticated computer technology available, this book will provide strategies to enable you to publish a newsletter that gets read.

A newsletter's success depends on your efforts in three specific areas: management of the newsletter process, selection and editing of the content, and high-impact newsletter design. The three sections of this book correspond to these crucial areas. You'll follow the newsletter process from inception to copy writing, from editing to design and the eventual distribution.

Section One covers the management of the newsletter process. You'll learn how to identify your objectives, set realistic budgets and production schedules, reach multiple audience segments with one newsletter, and conduct audience surveys that provide you with meaningful data.

Section Two discusses content that gets read. You'll see what distinguishes content that gets read from content that does not, and learn how to make sure the content you write grabs and keeps your readers' interest. You'll also learn about reliable techniques to help you write faster, as well as editorial shortcuts and strategies to integrate design and content.

Section Three details high-impact newsletter design. You will determine your newsletter's overall look by making decisions about eight static design elements. You'll learn how you can anticipate your reader's response based on the design decisions that you make. Whether to change your design is also discussed, along with how and when to do so. Section Three also gives you professional tips for using clip art and photographs which will add life and excitement to your newsletter.

Whether you're just beginning the process or have years of experience, you'll pick up tips, techniques, strategies, and shortcuts that you'll be able to use in your newsletter now and for years to come.

Jane K. Cleland

SECTION ONE:
THE MANAGEMENT OF
THE NEWSLETTER PROCESS

In this section, we'll analyze why some newsletters succeed and see how you can apply these principles of success. The first set of examples helps you identify achievable objectives, survey your audience, set a realistic production schedule, and budget with confidence. You'll see that with a solid foundation based on a clear objective and accurate reader information, generating copy and creating designs become easier and more straightforward. Furthermore, when you allocate resources within realistic parameters, your time and budget are more efficiently used to create newsletters that will succeed.

CONNECT TO YOUR AUDIENCE

Highlight content of specific and immediate interest to readers. Consider flagging their attention with a personal note or remark.

When newsletters are crisply written, tightly edited, and effectively designed, they succeed. In fact, newsletters are among the most powerful of all written media because when they're done well, there's a good likelihood they'll get read.

In order for your newsletter to succeed, you have to have a clear vision of why you're publishing one and you have to know a lot about the readers you're trying to reach. Think of the newsletter as the bridge between your objectives and your readers' interests and expectations.

To get the resources you need to do it right, whether it's time, an increase to your budget, or access to freelancers, you have to be able to demonstrate that your newsletter is working. You'll be able to use research that's been done by others and learn how you can do your own. These findings will either help you prove that your newsletter is working or show you why it isn't working so that you can fix it.

A local travel agency gives an example of clear vision and connecting with the reader.

Around The World with Donna Lee

Lorem ipsum dolor sit amet, consectetuer adipiscing elit, sed diam nonummy nibh euismod tincidunt ut laoreet dolore magna aliquam erat volutpat. Ut wisi enim ad minim veniam.

| SPE Publications Inc. | Volume 8, Number 1 | 123 Main Street, Anywhere, USA |
| | Spring/Summer 1996 | 303-111-4545 |

"LOREM IPSUM DOLOR SIT AMET, CONSECTETUER ADIPISCING ELIT, SED DIAM NONUMMY NIBH—EUISMOD TINCIDUNT UT LAOREET DOLORE MAGNA ALIQUAM ERAT " nisl ut aliquip ex ea commodo consequat. "DUIS AU V DOLOR" in hendrerit in vulputate velit esse molestie consequat, vel ill

WHY NOT BE IN EUROPE THIS SUMMER?

tincidunt ut laoreet dolore magna aliquam erat volutpat. Ut wisi enim ad minim veniam, quis nostrud exerci tation ullamcorper suscipit lobortis nisl ut aliquip ex ea commodo consequat. Duis autem vel eum iriure dolor in hendrerit in vulputate velit esse molestie consequat, vel ill um dolore eu feugiat nulla facilisis at vero eros et accumsan et iusto odio dignissim qui blandit praesent luptatum zzril delenit augue duis dolore te feugait nulla facilisi. Lorem ipsum dolor sit amet, consectetuer adipiscing elit, sed diam nonummy nibh euismod tincidunt ut laoreet dolore magna aliquam erat volutpat.

Ut wisi enim ad minim veniam, quis nostrud exerci tation ullamcorper suscipit lobortis nisl ut aliquip ex ea commodo consequat.   Duis autem vel eum iriure dolor in hendrerit in vulputate velit esse molestie consequat, vel illum dolore eu feugiat nulla facilisis at vero eros et accumsan et iusto odio dignissim qui blandit praesent luptatum zzril delenit augue duis

dolore te feugait nulla facilisi. Nam liber tempor cum soluta nobis eleifend option congue nihil imperdiet doming id quod mazim placerat facer possim assum. Lorem ipsum dolor sit amet, consectetuer adipiscing elit, sed diam nonummy nibh euismod tincidunt ut laoreet dolore magna aliquam erat volutpat.

Ut wisi enim ad minim veniam, quis nostrud exerci tation ullamcorper suscipit lobortis nisl ut aliquip ex ea commodo consequat. Duis autem vel eum iriure dolor in hendrerit in vulputate velit esse molestie consequat, vel illum dolore eu feugiat nulla facilisis. Duis autem vel eum iriure dolor in hendrerit in vulputate velit esse molestie consequat, vel illum dolore eu feugiat nulla facilisis. iriure dolor in hendrerit in vulputate velit esse molestie consequat, vel illum dolore eu feugiat nulla facilisis.

Bon Voyage

Lorem ipsum dolor sit amet, consectetuer adipiscing elit, sed diam nonummy nibh euismod tincidunt ut laoreet dolore magna aliquam erat volutpat. Ut wisi enim ad minim veniam, quis nostrud exerci tation ullamcorper suscipit lobortis nisl ut aliquip ex ea commodo consequat. Duis autem vel eum iriure dolor in hendrerit invulputate velit esse molestie consequat, vel illum dolore eu feugiat nulla facilisis at vero eros et accumsan et iusto odio dignissim qui blandit praesent luptatum zzril delenit augue duis dolore te feugait nulla facilisi.

Lorem ipsum dolor sit amet, consectetuer adipiscing elit, sed diam nonummy nibh euismod tincidunt ut laoreet dolore magna aliquam erat volutpat.Ut wisi enim ad minim veniam, quis nostrud exerci tation ullamcorper suscipit lobortis nisl u

t aliquip ea commodo velit esse molestie nsequat. facilisis at vero eros et accumsan et iusto odio digniss

Donna, a travel agent, is a good example of a publisher whose newsletter works because she has a clear vision of her purpose in publishing a newsletter. Donna's objectives are to sell her travel services and to build long-term relationships with clients by positioning herself as their "travel expert." In order to achieve these objectives, she sends the newsletter to people who are likely to be interested in her expertise.

Whenever Donna meets someone she thinks might be interested in her newsletter, she sends them a copy. She also sends it to people she has read about who she thinks might have an interest in travel. In the blank space on her nameplate she writes a personal note like, "Thought you'd be interested in the article on page 2. Regards, D." or "Take a look at the cost-cutting strategy on page 4. Best Wishes, D."

The note writing paid off in a big way. Donna read an article in the *New York Times* about a man who traveled extensively for his job, so she sent him a copy of her newsletter. The note in the nameplate said, "Enjoyed the *Times* article. Thought this would be of interest. Regards, D." She didn't hear a word for 18 months, then she got a call. "You seem to know a lot about the

Caribbean," he said. "I'm trying to go there for Christmas with my family and everything is sold out. Then I came across your newsletter, and it occurred to me, you might be able to help." Donna not only got the tickets, but hand-delivered them. She is now one of the official providers of travel for his company, a multinational corporation.

Donna was fortunate, because newsletters are usually read and then thrown away. Still, you can enjoy the same success as Donna if you follow the same two key principles: *Send your newsletter to people who want to get it, and tell them what they want to know.*

Donna's handwritten notes are a smart strategy, because handwriting is compelling and gets read more than other, more conventional fonts. By writing a personal note in the nameplate Donna

is accomplishing several things at once. She is customizing the newsletter, focusing the reader's attention on a key element, and making sure that at least some of the content gets read. At the same time, she is reminding them of who she is and making them feel part of the group.

Take a look at these two examples. It's easy to see that the handwritten note will be read first, and that it's likely to be read by more people than text that is set conventionally.

> **Enjoyed the *Times* article. Thought this would be of interest. Regards, D.**

Some of you may not have the time to handwrite a personal note on each newsletter. But if the idea appeals to you, you might consider having a part-time worker come in for a few hours a week to do the handwriting for you. If your newsletter has a properly focused objective, and you can demonstrate that you are achieving that objective, it may be possible to justify that kind of expense.

PURPOSE AND OBJECTIVES

Start thinking about your newsletter's objective by focusing on a one- or two-word statement of purpose. Words like *inform, educate, motivate, lobby, raise funds,* and *persuade* are commonly used. Once your purpose is set, then convert it to an objective by asking yourself, "What action do I want my reader to take as a result of reading my newsletter?"

Clearly, the winning combination is a compelling objective connected to a clear understanding of your readers' interests. The best objectives have both a narrow focus and an action orientation. They spring from a one- or two-word purpose. Typical purposes include *to educate, to inform, to motivate,* or *to sell*. Other purposes might include lobbying, fund-raising, or persuading.

Narrow down the purpose! One way to think of this is to ask yourself what action you hope your readers will take as a result of reading your newsletter. For example, "to educate" might translate into "to receive fewer questions from our customers on the hot-line emergency service number." The purpose is a general statement of intention, while the objective has a very narrow focus and answers the question, "How can I tell if it's a success?" Using the same formula, "to motivate" might become "to increase participation at the committee meetings so we always have a quorum." And "to raise funds" might evolve into "to raise enough money to allow all of the students to go on field trips all year."

Setting a clear and accurate objective is the critical first step in the newsletter publishing business, and it's deceptively complex. Consider long and hard before establishing your objectives. A woman in Houston, who worked for a nonprofit community organization, was having trouble pinpointing her newsletter's objective. When asked why she published a newsletter, she said that her organization wanted to inform the community of their services. When asked to explain further, she hesitated. Then, after a few moments, she said, "So that the members of the community will take advantage of our services, so taxpayers will feel their tax dollars are well-spent, and so people who don't need our services will know they exist if and when they do need them."

By pinpointing her newsletter's objectives so clearly and exactly, she will be better able to produce content that achieves that objective. Not only will her newsletter's copy be more on target, but the photographic subject matter will be more appropriate, too. In fact, defining her purpose so precisely can only help the newsletter, and the organization it represents, to succeed.

A recent study monitored how people read material in various formats. People scan magazines. (Seventy-five percent of readers read magazines from the back to the front.) However, people skim newspapers. They read the headline and the first paragraph, then skim the rest. Fewer than 20 percent of readers will follow a jumped article (one that says "continued on page 12"), and of those 20 percent, fewer than 3 percent will finish the article. But when people pick up a newsletter, they read it. In fact, there's a better chance they will finish it than if the same content was in any other form.

Because newsletters are read more often and with greater loyalty than other formats, they can serve to create a sense of identity for you or your organization.

SURVEYS

Whether you're first starting your newsletter or trying to capitalize on your loyal readership, it's a good idea to find out what your readers are thinking. There are many ways to survey an audience, but first consider how often you need to survey them. If your readership is fairly stable and unchanging, then you don't need to survey them often. If you have the budget and the access to technology, however, frequent surveying allows you to stay in touch with your audience's needs. The California Association of CPAs randomly selects 600 names (out of a circulation of 30,000) each quarter to survey. One of the things they learned early on from the surveys was that their readers wanted information on how the Internet could be of value to them, so they established a regular column on the subject called "Web Corner." It doesn't matter if the survey is part of the newsletter, in advance of publication, or an insert in the newsletter. What does matter is that it's short and easy to complete, and that questions are phrased in a way that encourages honest answers and elicits useful information.

web.corner

This is a spot for us to put in new and cool Web addresses to keep all of you wired. Most of them will be business related, but we will put some fun stuff on to keep you entertained.

- www.calcpa.org — The Society's Web site has news and information about state committees, all the chapters and more.
- Extra text to fill space. Extra text here to fill the page. Extra text here to fill the page. Extra text here to fill the page.

- Extra text here to fill the page. Extra text here to fill the page. Extra text here to fill the page. Extra text here to fill the page.
- Extra text here to fill the page. Extra text here to fill the page. Extra text here to fill the page. Extra text here to fill the page. Extra text here to fill the page. Extra text here to fill the page. ◆

Notice how the spider web graphic makes a pun of the word web, and its position in a corner cleverly connects it to the standing head. White space serves to counterbalance the unusual right corner placement of the graphic.

MAIL SURVEYS

Mail surveys are the most common type of survey. They'll allow you to keep up with your readers on a steady basis. You can expect the highest response from those surveys which are the easiest for your readers to complete. A recent survey was published with a headline which read: "20-Second Quality Check." This kind of heading assures the reader that the survey will be quick and easy.

The mail survey should probably be on one side of an 8½ x 11 sheet of paper. Directions for filling it out and instructions on folding, taping, and returning it to you should be included. Put your return address in the center panel on the reverse side of the paper. Always preprint your address, whether it's a full address with postal code and country name, or internal with your mailstop or office number, because that makes it easier for the recipients to return it.

Don't worry about **readability** in a mail survey. The idea here is for it to catch the eye in the in-basket or on the kitchen counter. So go ahead and print it on chartreuse or neon yellow paper (but be careful to test how it reproduces if you're asking them to fax it back). Consider using e-mail if that is an option for your readers.

Surveys use two kinds of questions: closed-ended and open-ended. Closed-ended questions are those which can be answered with one or two words (yes/no, rankings, multiple choice, or true/false). Open-ended questions solicit the respondent's opinion. "What would you like to read about in the newsletter?" or "What would you like to tell us about the newsletter?" are examples of open-ended questions.

You will generate a higher response from closed-ended questions. However, it's probably a good idea to ask some open-ended questions, because you want to find out exactly what your readers feel and think. A good rule for most mail surveys is to use no more than one or two open-ended questions per ten closed-ended. On a one-page survey, you might have four or five closed-ended questions and one open-ended question.

If the mailing list includes fewer than 500 people, you should probably survey them all. If the list includes more than 500, you might consider surveying a random sample, an "nth" sort (every fifth or eighth name, for example) to ensure a truly random mix.

A frequently asked question is, "What kind of a response can I expect from the survey?" There is no easy way to answer this question. It depends on the level of interest of your readers, the ease of completing the survey, timing, and a little luck, because there are so many variables. An editor of an industry association newsletter recently received a 30 percent response to a faxed survey from the members of her association. Most editors report a response rate closer to five percent or even less. Another organization's newsletter actually got an 87 percent response and the editor was disappointed! They were surveying technical school students and built the newsletter survey questions into a financial aid form, and they were surprised that 13 percent of students applying for aid skipped the newsletter survey questions.

Whether you rely on trend analysis (research done by others that reports on trends that may apply to your situation), or conduct extensive research yourself, knowing your readers' interests and expectations is a key to success with your newsletter.

U.S. Postage
PAID
Newsletter
Permit # 000

The Newsletter
123 Main Street
Anytown, USA 10203

Use this survey as a starting place. Think about what you want to know and how best to encourage reader participation. Don't feel that you have to use the same questions. This is intended to show you various question formats and styles as a starting place for you to begin thinking about what questions you should ask and how best to phrase them.

MAIL SURVEY

Instructions: *Help!* Please take two minutes to answer the following questions. This survey is self-addressed and post-paid, so when you're done, simply fold this sheet in thirds, tape it closed, and drop it in a mailbox. We appreciate your help.

1. I read every issue of *The Newsletter*.
   ☐ True   ☐ False

2. Rate each of the following attributes of *The Newsletter* as to how *interesting* it is.

	Highly	Moderately	Slightly	Not at all
Letter to the Editor	☐	☐	☐	☐
Classified advertising	☐	☐	☐	☐
Technical Update	☐	☐	☐	☐
Cartoons	☐	☐	☐	☐
Overall	☐	☐	☐	☐

3. In general, stories are: (check all that apply)
   ☐ Too long   ☐ About the right length   ☐ Superficial
   ☐ Often interesting ☐ Boring   ☐ Of limited interest to me
   ☐ Too hard to read ☐ Too hard to understand   ☐ Quick to read

4. I give my copy of *The Newsletter* to someone else when I'm done with it.
   ☐ Always   ☐ Often   ☐ Sometimes   ☐ Never

5. I'd love to read about:

U.S. Postage
PAID
Newsletter
Permit # 000

The Newsletter
123 Main Street
Anytown, USA 10203

THE EDITORIAL ADVISORY BOARD

You should have an active Editorial Advisory Board to help you stay in touch with your readers' needs and interests. Let me give you some specific suggestions about how to create one and work with one, and about how this Board can help you.

The Board should be made up of no more than eight people, and they should comprise a representative mixture of your readers. For example, if you are a manufacturing company, you might want someone from shipping, someone from finance, a quality expert, a marketing person, and you. If you are a church, you might want the pastor, the secretary, two parents, and a youth group member.

Ideally, the Board will meet for an hour to an hour and a half twice a year. They should be a group of people devoted to your cause and available to answer questions and make suggestions. The Board is also a means to help keep you in close touch with all the various constituencies the newsletter is representing.

Treat the Board members with a certain formality. It should be considered an honor to be on your Board. Give them credit on the masthead and appoint them for a specific term (maybe three years). You can always reappoint those who provide productive input.

Stay in constant touch with the Board. When a formal meeting is impossible, communicate with them via phone, fax, and e-mail. Keep several questions in mind that you want to ask them during calls or meetings so that you can work each one into the conversation.

Consider asking for their opinions about:

- articles you've run
- proposed articles
- the design of the newsletter
- its readability

Also ask them to survey their associates to broaden your feedback.

Anything you can do to help the Editorial Advisory Board function as a group will help your newsletter succeed, so consider offering coffee and muffins, a formal luncheon, T-shirts which read "I'm on _____'s Newsletter Advisory Board," and the like. Try to allocate budget dollars sufficient to send your Board members birthday cards. And be sure to thank them often for their efforts on your behalf.

Call on your Board throughout the year to get immediate feedback and guidance and to ensure that they feel connected to the newsletter process.

```
To:   Members of the Acme Newsletter Editorial Board
From: Sally Chen, Editor
Re:   Agenda
_____

1.   Two new Recurring Column ideas:  reaction and suggestions
2.   Shall we expand to 8 pages?
3.   New printer negotiations, preliminary budget data.
4.   Is the classified column working?
```

SATISFYING MULTIPLE AUDIENCES

You've analyzed your audience — now what? In an ideal world, you would have one newsletter for each segment of your audience, but that's not realistic for most publishers. Probably the next best alternative is to have a generic outside and a one-page insert specific to each audience segment.

Even though you have only one newsletter, don't assume that all your readers have the same interests. For example, the Justice Department employs three types of employees: lawyers, paralegals, and clerical workers. Rather than try to have each article satisfy all readers, the department's newsletter gives one story three ways, with three different slants. In one issue a **headline** read, "Lawyers: Good News! Research will be turned around quicker with new software installed in-house." Next to that story was an article that read, "Paralegals: Good News! Less travel time with more research done in-house!" And below that was an article that said: "Clerical Workers: Bad News — Computers down on Tuesday while new software is installed." The headlines serve to inform each group about which of the articles is relevant to them.

More of your newsletter will get read if you use this strategy than if you write as if all of your readers are alike. An

added benefit is that articles are shorter when they are written in this way, and shorter articles mean increased readership.

The California Association of CPAs had another good approach. Their membership, which totals 30,000, is made up of three distinct categories of workers: people who have passed the exam and are in their apprenticeship period, working CPAs, and retired CPAs. In a question and answer column, a retired CPA was asked, "What one thing do you know now that you wish you'd known when you started your career?"

This question reaches all three groups of readers. It communicates to the retirees that their experience and knowledge are valued. The CPAs just starting their careers get mentoring and guidance of real significance and depth. And the working accountants get advice as well as the message that their opinions will count in the future.

One name that's been suggested for this column is "Silver Pearls." Whether they select this or another name, it will be designed to invite readers in.

Once you've identified why you're publishing a newsletter, established the objectives which reflect the overall strategy, and analyzed your audience, you are ready to set a production schedule and create a budget.

PRODUCTION SCHEDULES AND BUDGETS

Add 20 percent to your estimate for all resources you need to produce the newsletter. If you expect the printer to take 10 days, for example, for scheduling purposes, call it two weeks. This will help you ensure that deadlines and budgets are met, and that any glitches are identified early on in the process.

The most effective way to create a production schedule is to start from the publication drop date or release date and work backwards. For example, let's say you want the newsletter distributed on August 10.

If you're mailing it by bulk mail, you probably want to allow three weeks for delivery, but you should add 20 percent more to protect you from emergencies like the printer's press breaking or a lost shipment. That means you have to get the newsletter to the lettershop by the 12th or 13th of July.

If it takes one day for delivery to the lettershop, increase it to two. That means that the printer has to be ready to ship the newsletter to the lettershop on the 9th of July. And if the printer needs ten days to print, dry, and fold the newsletter, you should increase it to 12 days.

				PRODUCTION SCHEDULE			
CHAMPION	TASK			START DATE	COMPLETE DATE	ACTUAL LEAD TIME	PREFERRED LEAD TIME
	Newsletter due						
Jim C	Distribution						
Bonnie B	Printing						
Bonnie B	Blueline proofing						
Brian L	Art to printer						
Brian L	Art production & proofing						
Brian L	Mock-up approval						
Brian L	Design & layout approval						
Brian L	Gather artwork/photography						
Kelly D	Editing						
John S	Writing copy						
Christa I	Story selection						

Following this logic, you have to deliver **camera ready** copy to the printer June 30. If it takes your office a day to proofread it, make it two. If you add a week for editing (based on a normal four-day turnaround), and another week to write it and one to assign stories and find reprints, you have to begin the newsletter no later than mid-June in order to make an August 10 deadline.

But what if a two-month production schedule is unrealistic? Then you zero in on all of the built-in extra time by beating your own deadlines where possible. You should also schedule those things that you can in advance.

As you complete the schedule, be sure to include only the steps which you really follow. The production schedule is a reality-based tool. Wishful thinking has no place in it. Also be aware that sometimes functions overlap. For example, you might be editing while someone else is scanning the photos into the system.

Budgets work in much the same way. Once you've created the production schedule, estimate the costs, again adding 20 percent at each step along the way.

As you rank expenditures, consider your objective and your audience's needs. If you're deciding on an 11 x 17 spread, you need a full-size monitor so you can view the two facing pages simultaneously. If you're feeling frustrated by your word processing program's inability to manipulate text well, perhaps it's time to upgrade to a page layout program.

Don't undervalue a professional's work. Yes, it may cost $100 or more to have a photograph taken, but if the photo grabs the audience's attention and therefore helps the newsletter to be read, many people would consider the fee well spent.

Your management tools are now complete. You've identified your objective, targeted your specific audience, set a sensible production schedule, and created a realistic budget. Now you're ready to develop content that will grab and hold your readers.

SECTION TWO:
CONTENT THAT GETS READ

Newsletters get read when the content is relevant and meaningful to the readers; therefore, careful consideration of what content to include in your newsletter is important. This section explains the implications of some current research for newsletter content, so that you will be better able to make appropriate choices for your publication and its readers.

ESTABLISHING CONTENT

Content is more important than design. It isn't that design doesn't matter — it does. However, design enhances the content, not the other way around. No one reads a newsletter simply because it's beautiful. Newsletters get read because they contain content people want.

The International Association of Business Communicators (the IABC) surveyed 45,000 readers of employee newsletters. They found that readers were interested in articles that related directly to them and that they preferred reading "news" rather than personal tidbits. While this research was specific to employee newsletters, the data can be applied to all newsletters.

The Newsletter Association conducted research into the relationship between the renewal rates of paid circulation newsletters and the inclusion of hard news. The study found that in newslet-

WHAT READERS WANT TO KNOW	
Managers	**Non-managers**
1. Product quality	1. The company's future
2. Cutting labor and other production costs	2. The competition
3. The company's future	3. Reasons behind the company's actions
4. Keeping up with technology	4. Organizational goals
5. Product development	5. Opportunities for career advancement
6. Compliance with regulations	6. Product development
7. Product liability	7. Employee benefits
8. Protecting the environment	8. The organization's strength and stability
9. Global competition	9. Product quality and quality-improvement efforts
10. Employee drug abuse	10. The organization's financial results

ters which were 100 percent hard news, such as stock and investment newsletters like the Kiplinger-Washington Report, renewal rates tended to be over 80 percent. When newsletters included features and other softer items, like portraits of industry leaders, along with the news, the renewal rates dropped to 60 percent. When newsletters included how-to information, the renewal rates dropped even further, to 50 percent. It's difficult to succeed with how-to information; if you offer advanced con-

tent you'll overwhelm beginners, but if you only offer the basics, you'll lose more accomplished people. The trick is to offer a balance of clearly differentiated basic and advanced content.

The overall findings of both surveys suggest that newsletters which include hard news to the exclusion of everything else have the most devoted readers. While this is true, it is not necessary to completely exclude "personal" news stories, cartoons, and jokes from

Notice that the top 10 content items include news items like productivity tips, the company's future plans, job advancement possibilities, and so on. Not included on the list are personal news items like birthdays, bowling scores, cartoons, jokes, or crossword puzzles.

your newsletter. Cartoons and jokes create a lively appearance and foster a lighthearted mood which may be exactly the image you want. Also, setting aside a section of the newsletter for personal news, usually in the back of the newsletter and not highlighted, encourages your readers to participate by submitting stories, photos, or anecdotes about themselves and others. They feel even closer to the newsletter when they later read the stories and see the photos they submitted.

Defining news

Since it is the "news" part of your newsletter which will be of most interest to your readers, it is crucial that you know what "news" means to them. Being aware of their needs, interests, and concerns enables you to select the articles which will be most relevant and timely for them.

News is *current* information which is *directly relevant* to your readers.

Focus on *your* readers, and the newsletter will be read. Consider this: A 78-year-old woman who lived in a nursing home published a newsletter for her fellow residents.

In one issue, there was an article about new furniture being delivered to the solarium, informing the residents when they could start entertaining visitors there. Another piece eased the readers' worries about twisted ankles by letting them know that a cracked sidewalk was being repaired. Also included was the résumé of the new nutritionist and the location of a sign-up sheet for her consultations. In just one newsletter, the publisher gave her audience current and detailed news about their lives and health.

The newsletter was successful because the articles were 100 percent hard news which was relevant to her readers. Her publication was just a simple, mimeographed sheet of paper, but what it lacked in glamour, it more than compensated for in newsworthy articles.

FEATURE ARTICLE STYLES

When you publish too infrequently to have information that is current, when you lack enough timely information, or when you need to write about the same information over and over again, you need to create a "feature." A feature is information that is relevant, but not timely.

For instance, a newsletter might run a news story about a revised 401(k) plan which asks employees to fill out a form. Because of low reader response, the story must be repeated as a feature to persuade readers who have not yet complied to fill out the form and send it in.

Features can be written in various styles. Below are descriptions of five feature styles: 5 W's, interview, first person, extended dialogue, and question and answer.

The 5 W's

The 5 W's answer the questions who, what, where, when, and why. In the example above, the story about the new 401(k) form has already been written as news. The next story might be told from the perspective of "who." For example, the focus could be on the person in Human Resources who is responsible for coordinating compliance. An article with a "why" focus could explore why the plan is administered in Human Resources and not handled by each separate department. Each "W" slant reintroduces the 401(k) form and thereby reinforces the original objective of the news article.

Some writers also use "how" as a device for creating features. "How" helps you analyze a process or evaluate a system.

The 5 W's Worksheet

Topic:

Key contacts: _____ phone # _____
_____ phone # _____
_____ phone # _____

Who:

When:

Where:

What:

Why:

If you fill out one of these forms for every news story, you'll be ready to develop features as needed.

The trick to conducting an effective interview is preparation. Begin by deciding on the first question you want to ask and then anticipate the answers. Think about what follow-up questions you might ask for each possible response you might receive. The more complete the question and answer flow chart, the better the interview will be.

The interview

The most effective approach to interviewing is to research your subject by gathering background information and knowing what you want to ask. This means getting your thoughts in order, anticipating reactions, and being organized. When you are not prepared, you may need to formulate your next question while the person you're interviewing is answering your last one, which may cause you to miss something.

The first-person article

The first-person approach establishes an emotional connection with the reader. This style is also useful when you want to create a feeling of empathy.

Imagine that you publish a newsletter for a computer software firm and there is a bug in its best-selling program. You are asked, as the company's newsletter editor, to include an article about the problem in every issue for the next three months. You might start an article by including the reader in the drama and tension of the situation: "You won't believe what I saw. First the screen went dark, then the signal came ...."

The 401(k) article, written from the first-person perspective, could start with a quote from an employee who has already sent in his form: "Maybe you are willing to wait, but not me. I'm due to retire soon, so I wasn't willing to delay at all." Both articles forge an emotional connection to the reader by using the word "you" before use of the personal pronoun "I."

Extended conversation

This format relies primarily on quotes. An extended conversation feature about a new interactive computer system designed to involve kids in a

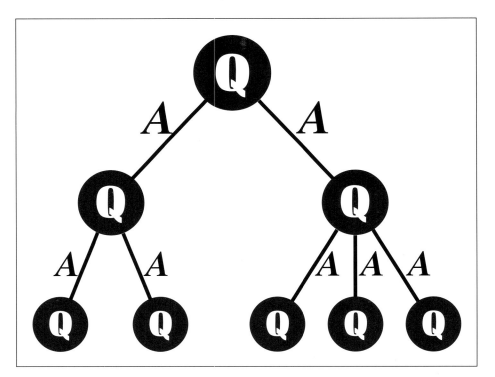

"It was great! I liked the fossil part best."

— Suzy Westerly, 8 years old

"Suzy liked the fossils. I liked the butterfly. It was so big!"

— LaVerna Hamal, 9 years old

"We consulted teachers, parents, and, of course, the kids themselves before we created the exhibit."

— Mary Jones, Curator

"I was scared about the computer, but it's very easy to use and the kids love it."

— Peter Lee, Docent

"My son came home so excited! This exhibit may have changed his life."

— John Peterson, Parent

"I asked to go back and my mom said yes."

— Suzy Westerly, 8 years old

science museum's exhibit might read as shown in the example to the left.

In the extended conversation method, instead of a long narrative article, there are smaller bite-sized pieces. Since short is always better than long in a newsletter, this is an effective means to condense your writing into an article more likely to be read.

Extended dialogue is well-received by readers. You have to be careful from a design point of view to ensure that each quote looks different from the others. You could put one quote in bold letters and another in italics and vary the fonts and color of the others. Use no more than two fonts, because small variations will serve your purpose better. The goal is to create different looks that nonetheless look harmonious, professional, and well-designed.

Question and answer

The question and answer format gives you control of the wording of the questions. Which question would you rather read: "Do you want to know about tax forms?" or "Do you want to know some strategies to save money on your taxes?" The first question is merely a dull invitation, but the second question entices the readers by telling them they might prosper from reading the answer. A question like, "Do you want to know what your liability is when you cross the state line?" is passive and does not move your reader to action. A question such as, "How can I avoid liability when I cross a state line?" involves the reader in the issues of their rights and responsibilities. The way to frame a successful question is to offer strategies to avoid negative outcomes or to focus on positive issues.

The question and answer format is especially effective for positioning bad news so readers are more likely to acquire the knowledge they need to deal with situations that might arise. Consider this popular format alternative if you have procedural changes, regulations, technical updates, or other news of limited appeal (no matter how important). By phrasing questions well — avoiding negative outcomes or accentuating the positive — you have a better chance of getting key information through the barriers readers put up.

When you design a question and answer article, make sure the Q's look different from the A's. It is important for your reader to see at a glance that the Q's are distinct and easy to read. Readers are more likely to read the Q's if they're easy to distinguish from the A's. And they'll gladly read the A's if they're interested.

Question?	Helvetica
Answer:	Times
Question?	Tekton
Answer:	Avant Garde
Question?	Freestyle Script
Answer:	Bookman
Question?	Futura
Answer:	Goudy Italic

CONTENT DEVELOPMENT

Searching for content that readers want to read about is a challenge many newsletter editors face. It's easy to drop into a routine that lets your newsletter stagnate. At times, you may feel that there's no new information "out there" for you to share with your readers. The truth is, there's plenty of it. While the content might not always be original, it can be collected, gathered, and written from various sources and perspectives. Here are some suggestions for places to find content.

Adaptations from other newsletters

Why reinvent the wheel each time you're searching for new content? Other newsletters can be an excellent source of ideas for your own readership. Don't be bound by the fact that other newsletters are different from yours or that their readership is unlike yours. By collecting and searching through other newsletters, you can provide yourself with endless ideas for articles which could prove interesting to your own readers as well.

A good example comes from a newsletter published by the National Catholic Educational Association, which ran a quiz challenging their target readers. The quiz tested readers' aptitude for Catholic school administration. Quizzes are involving, and when the questions are phrased properly, they are a tool to educate as well. You could identify an ideal, a goal, or a vision that would interest your readers and develop it into an interactive quiz. For instance, "Do You Have What It Takes to Be an International Traveler?" or "Do You Have the Personality Traits of an Ideal School Board Member?" Editorial Eye ran an article called "Profile of an Excellent Editor." Can you see how this is the same idea?

Whatever the group you are trying to target, a quiz is an excellent way of reaching them, involving them, and educating them.

When a phone company bid on a job and lost to an alternative carrier, the company approached the man who had rejected their bid and asked if they could write a newsletter article about his decision. The article was titled, "Lou: The One Who Got Away." This concept converts a negative into a positive. A strategy for adapting this concept is going to your company's Personnel Office and asking them to discuss the reasons why employees quit. Or if your organization is a church or temple, you could write an article titled, "Why a Family Left Our Congregation."

Notice that in all these examples we are not highlighting any one individual. We're not trying to embarrass or humiliate anyone. In the phone company's newsletter, for instance, they didn't point fingers at employees; rather, they tried to show how a customer thinks, how the decision process evolves, all with an eye to improving their customer relationships. In this kind of article, we're asking ourselves, "What can we learn from this?"

Likewise, with the employee newsletter we're not looking to profile an employee who quit. Rather we're going to analyze *why* employees quit, and what we, the organization, can do to address these concerns, so that in the future turnover is reduced.

When you consider why a family leaves the church or temple, you're not focusing on a personality clash or one parent's disappointments with religious training. The point isn't to highlight individual issues. The point is to pinpoint trends, and address them; to reveal opportunities for success and ensure everyone in the community knows how to take advantage of them.

Here is an example of taking a negative and converting it to a positive that demonstrates the response tool approach very effectively: An herbal tea company discovered that their mint tea was not selling well in certain markets because some of their customers perceived the flavor of mint as medicinal. Articles in the company's newsletter targeting retailers set about reversing this opinion. They stressed the tea's refreshing, soothing qualities and set up an 800 number where retailers could order free mint tea bags as giveaways.

By assigning a dedicated phone number they could easily track response. They learned that a significant percentage of requests came from retailers reading the newsletter, not from salespeople's giveaways or other advertising efforts.

Building in response tools to your newsletter whenever you can is an effective way to see if the newsletter is working.

Upcoming events

Your own calendar of events is another source for article ideas. Pieces about future trade shows, budget deadlines, product introductions, etc. can be written in advance and used later in the appropriate issue.

While many people use "upcoming" articles as a way to promote an event, you may want to alter how you present this information. Upcoming events often have many natural extensions which can offer you possibilities for additional articles for your newsletter. For example, announcing a blood drive might spawn articles about readers who have previously benefited from blood donations in surgery or after an accident. Or, you

may want to write an article about common fears and myths of donating blood. The key is to hook your readers' interest, thereby subtly promoting an upcoming event.

800 numbers and 888 numbers are a good way to track response. Some voice mail systems allow you to dedicate an extension to the newsletter and easily track response. Whether you offer readers a promotional giveaway or invite their written, faxed, or e-mailed response, this approach is an excellent way for you to prove the newsletter's value.

News of the Night

VOLUME 1   August 1996

Safety Tips

1. Lorem ipsum dolor sit amet, consectetuer adipiscing elit, sed diam nonummy nibh euismod tincidunt.

2. Ut wisi enim ad minim veniam, quis nostrud exerci tation ullamcorper suscipit lobortis nisl ut aliquip ex ea commodo

New Options for Late Night Commuters

Nam liber tempor cum soluta nobis eleifend option congue nihil imperdiet doming id quod mazim placerat facer possim assum. Lorem ipsum dolor sit amet, consectetuer adipiscing elit, sed diam nonummy nibh euismod tincidunt ut laoreet dolore magna aliquam erat volutpat.

Ut wisi enim ad minim veniam, quis nostrud exerci tation ullamcorper suscipit lobortis nisl ut aliquip ex ea commodo consequat.

Duis autem vel eum iriure dolor in hendrerit in vulputate velit esse molestie consequat, vel illum dolore eu feugiat nulla facilisis.

Lorem ipsum dolor sit amet, consectetuer adipiscing elit, sed diam nonummy nibh euismod tincidunt ut laoreet dolore magna aliquam erat volutpat. Ut wisi enim ad minim veniam, quis nostrud exerci tation ullamcorper suscipit lobortis nisl ut aliquip ex ea commodo consequat.

Duis autem vel eum iriure dolor in hendrerit in vulputate molestie consequat, vel illum dolore eu feugiat nulla vero eros et accumsan et iusto odio dignissim qui aesent luptatum zzril delenit augue duis dolore te lla facilisi. Lorem ipsum dolor sit amet, consectetuer elit, sed diam lore magna enim ad minim uis nostrud on ullamcorper bortis nisl ut ea commodo . Duis autem ure dolor in n vulputate molestie con vero eros et accumsan et iusto odio dignissim qui aesent luptatum zzril delenit augue duis dolore te lla facilisi.

per tempor cum soluta nobis eleifend option congue rdiet doming id quod ma zim placerat facer possim rem ipsum dolor sit amet, consectetuer adipiscing diam nonummy nibh euismod tincidunt ut laoreet agna aliquam erat volutpat.

Ut wisi enim ad minim veniam, quis nostrud exerci tation

HELP! We're testing whether you're reading this newsletter.

Please call Jennifer at
555-5555
ext. 555

rem ipsum dolor sit amet, consectetuer
m
m
er
equat, vel illum dolore eu feugiat nulla

HELP! We're testing whether you're reading this newsletter.

Please call Jennifer at
555-5555
ext. 555

HELP!

Your ideas are needed. Submit story ideas to:

Loren ipsum sit, consecte Apiscing, IL

Mary submitted an idea to the Newsletter.

See yourself in print! Submit your ideas to Bob 555-4545 ext. 555

Contributions Welcome

Please send your story ideas to:

Loren ipsum dolor sit arnet, consectetuae Adipiscing, IL

WANTED

GOOD STORY IDEAS FOR OUR NEWSLETTER. SUBMIT E-MAIL OR LEAVE VOICE MAIL:

mary@e-mail.com
1•800•123•4567

Reader submissions

Asking your readers for ideas is the most direct way to both determine their preferences and generate content. A form requesting their story ideas, such as the 5 W's form, could be inserted in each issue. Sending a submission form in each issue gives your readers every chance to respond with their ideas and suggestions. Also, if you keep changing the color of the form, it will be more likely to catch their attention.

One common error to avoid is asking readers to keep the form. They won't do it. The truth is, people will only submit an idea when they have an idea — and if they happen to remember you want their submissions.

Put instructions at the top of the 5 W's form that say, for example:

Extra! Extra! Contributions Welcome! We'll do the writing, just tell us the facts. Take a minute and fill in this form. Send it to the mailstop below, and we'll do the rest. Look for your idea in an upcoming issue!

Notice that by asking readers to complete the 5 W's form, you get them to do much of the work for you — and yet you're positioning it as a relatively painless task.

A box that's located on the same page, saying the same thing, using the same fonts issue after issue becomes the visual equivalent of white noise. Your readers will not even notice it unless you vary the color, headlines, and text. Use a couple of different headlines. Make the box tall and skinny on page 3 of one issue, then put it in an elliptical shape on page 4 of the next, for example. You have to make sure it stands out; you have to catch your reader's eye.

Other sources for content

Sources for content are endless. Keep an eye out for any possible source of information: friends, family, school, magazines, television programs, billboards, bumper stickers, etc. Literally keep your eyes and ears open: Observe all that is around you and think of ways each piece of information you filter might be of interest to your readers.

Get a manila file folder and label it "Story Ideas," so you have a place to collect and retrieve them. You may choose to do this electronically; however, a file folder allows you the flexibility to rip and tear articles and put sticky notes on them. When you're searching for ideas, you'll always have a place to go to begin your brainstorming process.

Dialogue with members of your Editorial Advisory Board should be an ongoing source of pertinent content information. Use them as your additional eyes and ears. Don't feel as if you're "in this alone." Also, news based on up-to-the-minute research on industry trends provides content of enduring value to your readers. Finally, use the listing at right as a tool to jumpstart your thinking.

The story ideas listed here can be adapted to your needs and used over and over again. Also, they can be combined. For example, you could use No. 1, "Profile Leaders," combined with No. 10, "Enhance Decision-Making Skills," by conducting a series of interviews with the vice presidents in your company and asking them, "How do you make decisions?"

1. **Profile Leaders:** Interview a long-time employee, member, or customer; an industry giant; or a senior-level executive.

2. **Analyze Ethical Dilemmas:** Consider small issues your readers face on a daily basis (i.e., software piracy, photocopying cartoons) as well as decisions rendered by the court; create models for decision making; review the consequences of others' decisions.

3. **Report Industry Trends:** Reflect geographic, economic, or competitive factors and how they impact trends; what effect will new technology have on current conditions?

4. **How to Improve Listening Skills:** Focus on active listening; how physiology impacts listening ability; note taking as an aid to listening.

5. **Define Industry Jargon:** Use a glossary or a dictionary layout; explain the derivation of terminology or the use of acronyms.

6. **How to Be More Creative:** Describe right brain vs. left brain; explain free association; consider how mood affects creativity.

7. **Tips to Improve Quality:** Provide examples of continuous improvement; discuss empowerment; offer suggested approaches.

8. **Suggestions to Increase Productivity:** Focus on specifics of streamlining systems, ferreting out cost savings, working efficiently, identifying high-energy times of the day.

9. **Summarize Minutes of Various Meetings:** Executive board meetings; Board of Directors meetings; team meetings.

10. **Enhance Decision-Making Skills:** Discuss the difference between problems and symptoms of problems; rational vs. emotional decisions; the risk of inaction vs. the risk of action.

11. **Computer Shortcuts:** Highlight user-friendly approaches in all fields, from accounting and word processing to inventory control.

12. **Avoid Sexual Harassment:** Provide verbal and physical examples; offer case histories; review your organization's grievance procedures.

13. **Manage Stress Effectively:** Describe exercises which can be done while sitting down; meditation; enjoying humor.

14. **Time Capsule—A Return to the Past:** Explain the evolution of your organization's logo, mission statement, and/or current facility; the founder's vision; serendipitous events that led to the beginning, or that led to the current state of the organization.

15. **Reverse Time Capsule—Predict the Future:** If interest rates go up, how will that impact inventory control? What if the cost of recycling goes down?

16. **Reviews of Books, Movies, Videos, Software, etc.:** This is an especially effective way to involve specialists throughout your company. People love having their opinions solicited and seeing them in print.

17. **Overcome Your Fear of Public Speaking:** Ranked as people's number one fear, tips to overcome it will be welcome. How about articles on visualization, rehearsal, or handling questions?

18. **Be Prepared—Emergency Procedures:** Offer specific instructions in case of fire, flood, lightning, burns, shock.

19. **Calming Angry People:** Overcoming defensiveness, negotiating solutions, or specific vocabulary suggestions.

20. **We're in the News!** Reprint or summarize press coverage.

21. **Recycling Techniques and/or Policies:** Trace a plastic bottle from initial creation to its re-creation as something else; maybe trace the process from the original ingredients' mining or fabrication. Try paper, rubber, metal, or anything that's recycled.

22. **Get Your Message Across:** Business writing techniques, shortcuts, and strategies are always welcome.

23. **Using New Technology:** Demystifying technology is helpful to laypeople; in fact, explaining technology they don't themselves use, but which is relevant to the company, helps build a sense of shared purpose, and thus serves to improve morale.

24. **Trivia:** Look up the origins of your industry's terminology in dictionaries; or report on lore from your region, or the company headquarters' locale.

Calendar and event schedules

One element of content that should appear in every issue is a calendar or a schedule of events. A list of events is a kind of news article delivered in an orderly, organized fashion.

Whether presented in narrative or graphic form, the calendar should look the same and be positioned in the same place issue after issue.

There is no one ideal place for a calendar to be positioned, just so long as it's logical and accessible. For example, if you ask your readers to keep the calendar, it doesn't make any sense to print it on the reverse side of a survey you're asking that they return to you.

Focus on the facts. Highlight the 5 W's. What is the event you're promoting? When does it occur? Where? Who should attend? Why are you recommending it? Be consistent in your organization of information. If you always start with the date, for example, readers soon learn to search by this heading.

The following example illustrates the importance of calendars in newsletters: An engineer in Nashville, Tennessee, wanted to expand his business to

include residential architects. Part of his marketing plan was to publish a newsletter to be mailed to the architects. He wanted to prove his newsletter's effectiveness, so he used built-in response devices such as offering child-sized baseball caps and other giveaways. Every time someone called for a cap, he conducted an informal phone survey asking his audience, "What do you most value in the newsletter?" One hundred percent of them answered, "the calendar."

The calendar graphic can allude to your organization or company's business. For example, a school could publish a calendar that looks like a blackboard with chalk lettering. A computer company could center theirs on a monitor, or an accounting firm's calendar could appear on a ledger. If you're publishing a company newsletter, scan in the staff meeting agenda and use an icon of a thumbtack or a push pin to make it appear to be posted to a bulletin board.

Calendars are, by definition relevant and current; thus, they're an important form of news.

He found a way to create great reader loyalty. He contacted the U.S. Weather Service, which publishes a long-range weather forecast. It's free and in the public domain. He printed it under the heading "Construction Weather Forecast." His readers already had the same data from the same source, but didn't appreciate its value before, because it wasn't a *construction* forecast.

This demonstrates several key points: calendars which contain relevant, timely information (news) are highly valued; and perception matters more than reality. You must ensure that your readers perceive the value of your calendar. Also note that response devices can be used for surveying your readers, as well as for tracking response.

Your calendar is a static design element, so its look and location in the newsletter should not change. Do not put anything on the reverse side that is of equal value (such as a survey that you want returned to you).

Many newsletters are geared to multiple audiences, so it can be difficult to fashion a calendar to meet the needs of all the groups. Creating a key can help. Here's an example: The editor of a newsletter for a farmer's association

needed to reach four distinct groups: farmers, manufacturers of farming equipment, feederies, and universities with agricultural programs. Using a two-color format, she put an 18-point rule under each calendar entry and chose a different color for the rule for each group. This way she color-coded the calendar according to each group's activities.

Whether your calendar is simple and straightforward, or as fancy as some of the options mentioned earlier; low-tech or high-tech; fashioned for one audience or many; it is an important tool for capturing and holding your readers' interest.

1996 SUMMER EVENTS CALENDAR Downtown Civic Center

● **JUNE 6**
Sit amet, consectetur adipscing elit, sed diam nonnumy eiusmod tempor incidunt ut labore et dolore magna aliquam erat volupat.

▲ **JUNE 14-15**
Ut enim ad minimim veniami quis nostnud exercitation.

■ **JUNE 23**
Ullamcorpor suscipit laboris nisi ut aliquip ex ea commodo consequat. Duis autem vel eum irure dolor in reprehenderit in voluptate velit esse molestaie son consequat, vel illum dolore eu fugiat nulla pariatur.

● **JUNE 29-30**
At vero eos et accusam et justo odio dignissim qui blandit praesent lupatum delenit aigue duos dolor et molestais excepturi sint occaecat cupidat non provident, simil tempor sunt in culpa qui officia desenunt moll anim id est labonum et dolor fugai. Et harumd dereud facilis est er expedit distinct.

■ **JULY 1**
Sit amet, consectetur adipscing elit, sed diam nonnumy eiusmod tempor incidunt ut.

★ **JULY 7**
Ullamcorpor suscipit laboris nisi ut aliquip ex ea commodo consequat. Duis autem vel eum irure dolor in reprehenderit in voluptate velit esse molestaie son consequat, vel illum dolore eu fugiat nulla pariatur.

★ **JULY 14-17**
At vero eos et accusam et justo odio dignissim qui blandit praesent lupatum delenit aigue duos dolor et molestais excepturi sint occaecat.

● **JULY 24**
Nam liber a tempor cum soluta nobis eligend optio.

▲ **JULY 29**
Temporem autem quinsud et aur office deb aut tum rerum necessit atib saepe eveniet ut er repudiand sint et molestia.

■ **AUGUST 2**
Sit amet, consectetur adipscing elit, sed diam nonnumy eiusmod tempor incidunt ut labore et dolore magna aliquam erat.

● **AUGUST 12**
Ut enim ad minimim veniami quis nostnud exercitation.

★ **AUGUST 13**
Ullamcorpor suscipit laboris nisi ut aliquip ex ea commodo consequat.

■ **AUGUST 20-22**
At vero eos et accusam et justo odio dignissim qui blandit praesent lupatum delenit aigue duos dolor et molestais excepturi sint occaecat cupidat non providentt.

■ **AUGUST 28**
Nam liber a tempor cum soluta nobis eligend optio comque nihil quod a imped anim id quod maxim placeat facer possim omnis es voluptas assumenda omnis dolor repellend.

▲ **SEPTEMBER 5**
Sit amet, consectetur adipscing elit, sed diam nonnumy eiusmod tempor incidunt ut labore et dolore magna aliquam erat volupat.

● **SEPTEMBER 5**
Ut enim ad minimim veniami quis nostnud exercitation suscipit laboris nisi ut aliquip ex ea commodo consequat. Duis autem vel eum irure dolor in reprehenderit in voluptate velit esse molestaie son consequat, vel illum dolore eu fugiat nulla pariatur.

▲ **SEPTEMBER 5**
At vero eos et accusam et justo odio dignissim qui blandit praesent lupatum delenit aigue duos dolor et molestais excepturi sint occaecat.

★ **SEPTEMBER 5**
Culpa qui officia desenunt moll anim id est labonum et dolor fugai. Et harumd dereud facilis est er expedit distinct.

Students = ●   Businesses = ★   Universities = ■   Government = ▲

Recurring columns

Another key piece of content for newsletters is recurring columns. Recurring columns repeat in every issue. They help build morale and reader familiarity with your newsletter and its content. This type of column content should always look the same and appear under a **standing head.**

A standing head is a kind of title. It does not replace a headline. A title is a graphic device that helps the unit of content be recognized, while the headline serves to interest the reader in the column's content. Each column should have a standing head as well as a headline.

Typical standing heads include "Technical Update," "President's Letter," and "Member's News." The most effective recurring columns are those which contain factual news; the least effective are editorial columns.

If your boss insists on having a "President's Letter" even though such a column is generally quite unpopular with readers, there are things you can do to improve its chances of being read. Often the effective content is buried under a banal start like, "My, we've had a cold winter ..." or "Now that Thanksgiving is upon us ...." A well-written

headline can entice a reader to struggle through an unpromising beginning for the rewarding information that the headline promises.

Another tactic for getting to the valuable content is to cut the first two paragraphs of the column. The third paragraph is where useful information like profit potential, productivity changes, or reorganization often begins. This is the content that your readers probably want to know about.

Computer Update

COMPUTER UPDATE

Computer Update

Computer Update

With different fonts or simple graphics you can create very different looks for your standing heads. For example, use heavy, dark fonts and borders to convey a sense of power, use a script to convey a sense of elegance, and use graphic images, such as this computer, to connect the standing head to the content.

Standing heads are a good way to create a specific image. Use type and graphics to convey a mood while providing information.

A cleverly worded title can suggest that a column's content is relevant yet easy and quick to read. "WordPerfect User Tip of the Month" sounds brief and beneficial. "Technical Update" sounds timely, as does "Quality Flash." Both titles also suggest that they could be read rapidly. It is helpful to suggest the column's purpose in the title. If your readers want strategies to improve communication, create a column called "Communication Strategy." If they need information about the status of the capital drive for a new hospital wing, "Patient Care Capital Drive Update" is an apt title. "Works for Me" is a column that worked for a chain of health food stores. The column was devoted to customer testimonials about the chain's products. According to the editor, products featured in this column "flew" off the shelves.

A newsletter with multiple columns conveys a sense of unity. Recurring columns are recognizable and reassuring to the reader, and when there are many the entire newsletter gets a "familiar" look. One major publisher was testing a textbook series that used literature to teach children to read. The publisher's four-page, all-column newsletter united the teachers scattered across the country who were testing the textbooks, by addressing their issues and concerns.

The columns were entitled, "Art Teachers' Contributions," "Music Teachers' Sounding Board," "Parents' Ideas," etc. The newsletter conveyed practical advice while connecting the readers in a common purpose.

Reviews are another type of recurring column. They synthesize information and serve it up in quick, concise pieces. A manufacturing company's newsletter ran a "Restaurant Review" column to inform workers about nearby eateries.

Because of the column's popularity with readers, it was expanded into "Entertainment Review." Reviews of books, software, and the Internet are also well-received by readers.

Advertising

Paid advertising makes a newsletter look more like a magazine, and magazines are not as thoroughly read as newsletters. Therefore, if you choose to use advertising in your newsletter, be sure you design the advertising to be less commercial and more content- and information-oriented. Classified advertising, however, can be used effectively if it is perceived as a service. In order to achieve this effect, use a headline in addition to the standing head. For example, in the Spring issue, the headline might read: "Think Spring — Boats for Sale."

You're not limited to using any particular fonts. Although the text in a newsletter should be set in no more than two fonts, it's perfectly acceptable to use many more than that for standing heads.

Your material is protected whether you publish a notice of copyright or not. If you want to publish a notice that your material is protected, you should specify these three things: either the word "copyright" or the little letter "c" with a circle around it ©; the name of the owner of the copyright, whether that's you or your organization; and the year of first publication.

Copyright laws

Particularly if you are going to use articles or content from other sources, it is important that you have some understanding of copyright laws.

First of all, you must assume all published material is covered under the copyright laws. Giving attribution for a quote is not enough: Attribution is not the same as permission. Since the mid-80s, America, along with over 150 other countries, has been part of the Berne Convention. Under this convention, all these countries have agreed to adhere to the same standards of copyright protection.

You are fully protected under the law whether you publish a notice or not. Another option is to register formally with the Library of Congress. They are the official "keeper" of the copyright. If you ever need to prove date of publication, this registration will help.

By definition, only original works of authorship when fixed in a tangible form can be copyrighted. Specifically, ideas, facts, and statistics are not copyrightable. Headlines and titles are also not copyrightable, because their accessibility puts their originality into question. That's why you sometimes see the same title in different movies or books. Speeches are not copyrightable, but when a speech is backed up by a paper (as when a scholar delivers a paper at a conference), it is fully protected. A broadcaster's tape renders the presentation fully protected.

Adhering to the copyright law is the ethical thing to do. When you use someone else's material without their permission, you are robbing a creative person not only of their material, but of their right to decide where it appears. In addition, it's the law, and violation of copyright means that you're breaking the law. Also, getting caught can be extremely embarrassing.

A newsletter publisher in Washington, D.C., learned this the hard way. A member of his heavy industrial equipment association sent him a cartoon that was industry-specific and right on target, so he used it, without permission. One of the recipients of his newsletter happened to be the cartoonist who had created the cartoon. The cartoonist demanded, and received, a full-page apology in the newsletter. In addition, there were monetary damages, and a letter was placed in the editor's permanent personnel file.

There are certain instances when you can use copyrighted material without permission. A news summary is a specific exemption under the law. When a journalist says, "According to broadcast reports ..." or "According to written reports ..." they are allowed to quote from the original news source without permission.

"Fair use" allows a person to use copyrighted material without permission as long as the use falls within reasonable boundaries. Courts have held that companies engaged in profit-making activities can take far fewer liberties

© Owner, Year of 1st Publication

with "fair use" than nonprofit educational institutions engaged in scholarly research. But in all cases, a judge will consider the amount of copyrighted material you're using, its relative significance to the whole, and the impact the use of the material is likely to have on the future marketability of the original item.

For example, if you use a 50-word quote from a 500-page book in a book review, that might enhance sales of the book and the writer could profit. A judge would consider those aspects in your favor in determining fair use. However, if you use a 50-word quote from a 100-word article, you have used half of the copyrighted material, and prevented the writer from gaining profit through reprints.

Permission to use copyrighted material is almost always given when requested. While many aspects of the copyright laws are confusing, it is a very important issue. For further clarification, information, or copyright registration forms, contact the Library of Congress directly at (202) 707-9100 or (202) 707-3000, or write to:

Registrar of Copyrights
The Copyright Office
Library of Congress
Washington, D.C. 20559.

SIX TECHNIQUES TO GET YOUR NEWSLETTER READ

Once you've determined what content categories are most appealing to your readers, and you have a working draft of the content, there are six specific techniques that will help your newsletter get read. If you use all six, you'll dramatically increase the impact of your newsletter. Even using just two or three will help your newsletter get read.

Your goal in paragraphing is to create short sections of copy. Think bite-sized pieces.

Length

Everything about your newsletter should be short. The average sentence should be no longer than 20 words. An average of 17 words per sentence is even better. This means that if you write a 30-word sentence, you should balance it with a ten-word sentence.

Paragraphs should be no longer than seven to nine lines. Readers become intimidated by long units of copy, so the shorter your paragraphs, the more likely your articles will get read.

Stories should have no more than five to seven paragraphs. A typical line of text has approximately five words. If the length of the paragraph is the recommended seven lines, then the paragraph will contain about 35 words. Multiplying 35 words by seven para-graphs equals 245 words. Thus an ideal length for a newsletter article is about 250 words or fewer.

Sometimes it is difficult to keep news-letter articles under 250 words. When you must run longer articles, there are several strategies to make the copy look shorter and therefore more readable.

The first method is to sprinkle a lot of white space throughout the article by indenting paragraphs, increasing the space between lines and columns, and adding space around headlines. Second, well-written **subheads** placed every three or four paragraphs will also serve to divide the copy into smaller, reader-friendly segments.

Breaking up one lengthy article into two or more articles is another option for keeping articles a reasonable length. Make sure that each article is a cohesive unit able to stand alone, as it will be

Downtown News

Lorem ipsum dolor sit amet, consectetur adipscing elit, sed diam nonnumy eiusmod tempor incidunt ut labore et dolore magna aliquam erat volupat. Ut enim ad minimim veniami quis nostnud exercitation ullamcorpor suscipit laboris nisi ut aliquip ex ea commodo consequat. Duis autem vel eum irure dolor in reprehenderit in voluptate velit esse molestaie son consequat, vel illum dolore eu fugiat nulla pariatur. At vero eos et accusam et justo odio dignissim qui blandit praesent lupatum delenit aigue duos dolor et molestais exceptur sint occaecat cupidat non provi-dent, simil tempor sunt in culpa qui officia desenunt mollH anim id est labonum et dolor fugai. Et harumd dereud facilis est er expedit dis-tinct. Nam liber a tempor cum soluta nobis eligend optio comque nihil quod a impedH anim id quod maxim placeat facer possim omnis es voluptas assumenda est, omnis dolor repellend. Temporem autem quinsud et aur office debH aut tum rerum necessit atib saepe eveniet ut er repudiand sint et molestia non este recusand. Itaquitae earud renum hic tenetury sapiente delectus au aut pre-fer endis dolorib asperiore repellat. Hanc ego cum tene sentntiam, quid est cur verear ne ad eam non possing accommodare nost ros quos tu paulo ante cum memorite it tum etia ergat. Nos et amice et nebevol, eolestias access ptest fier ad augendas cum con-scient to factor tum toen legum odioque civiuda. Et tamen in busdad modut est neque ned libiding gen cupiditat, quas.

Downtown News

Lorem ipsum dolor sit amet, consectetur adipscing elit, sed diam nonnumy eiusmod tempor incidunt ut labore et dolore magna aliquam erat volupat. Ut enim ad minimim veniami quis nostnud exercitation ullamcorpor suscipit laboris nisi ut aliquip ex ea com-modo consequat. Duis autem vel eum irure dolor in reprehenderit in voluptate velit esse molestaie son consequat, vel illum dolore eu fugiat nulla pariatur. At vero eos et accusam et justo odio dignissim qui blandit praesent lupatum delenit aigue duos dolor et molestais exceptur sint occaecat cupidat non provi-dent, simil tempor sunt in culpa qui officia desenunt mollH anim id est labonum et dolor fugai. Et harumd dereud facilis est er expedit distinct. Nam liber a tem-por cum soluta nobis eligend optio comque nihil quod a impedH anim id quod maxim placeat facer pos-sim omnis es voluptas assumenda est, omnis dolor repellend. Temporem una autem quinsud et aur office debH aut tum rerum necessit atib saepe eveniet ut er repudiand sint cum recusand. Itaquitae earud renum hic tenetury sapiente delectus au aut prefer endis dolorib asperiore factor repellat. Hanc ego cum tene sentntiam, quid est cur verear ne ad eam non possing accommodare nost ros quos tu paulo ante cum memorite it tum etia ergat. Nosta et atimice et nebevol, eolestias access ptest fier ad augendas cum con-scient to factor tum ton legum odioque.

read independently from the others. Isolating categories of content within an article will help you to easily divide an article into multiple units.

Sidebars are another means of division. For example, a list of technical terms or jargon could be extracted from the main body of the article and placed in a sidebar. An added benefit of isolating the terms in a sidebar is that you are simultaneously making it easy for the newcomer to understand the material and speeding the experienced person's reading.

Even if an article is lengthy, try to avoid jumps. Jumping an article (asking the reader to turn to another page) lowers readership. It is always advantageous to print the entire article on one page.

Ease in reading

Ease in reading is another important factor to keep in mind when writing your newsletter. Unlike journals, technical reports, or abstracts, which aim to educate or instruct the reader, your newsletter must be readable in order to succeed.

First-time newsletter publishers are often startled when they learn that newsletters should be written at a sixth- to ninth-grade level. Keeping the lan-

guage at a level that is easily grasped and quickly understood is not done in an effort to condescend to the readers, but to present them with valuable information in a clear and accessible format. Most popular magazines are written at the seventh-grade level, and most college textbooks are written between the eighth- and ninth-grade levels. While this may seem astounding, keep in mind that you're publishing a newsletter — which by definition should be accessible and easy to read. People never notice writing that's easy, only writing that's too hard.

A major international publication conducted a study in which they asked 100 CEOs to evaluate three books. They were asked to judge the books on the basis of relevancy, usefulness, and hard-hitting impact. Ninety-nine of the executives chose one book as having those qualities, another book got the remaining vote, and the last book got no votes. The study revealed that it was the same book edited at three different reading levels. The book edited at the twelfth-grade level got no votes, the one edited at the ninth-grade level got one vote, and the book edited at the sixth-grade level got the 99 votes. This

research supports the idea that readers value material that is clearly and accessibly written.

> "Lorema ipsum dolorit sit amet, erata consectetur adipscing elit, sedet ediam nonnumy eiusod una tempor incidunt utas labore et dolore magna aliquam erat volupat. Ut enim ad minimal veniami quis nostnud et exercitation ullam corpor isuscipit laboris nisi ut aliquip extasulisa ea comodo end estas il coniquat."

Use pull-quotes (also called blurbs) to break up the layout and entice the reader into the article. A pull-quote takes a quote out of the context of the article and sets it aside graphically. This use of quotes can create interest, fill up extra space, and break up long sections of copy.

Adipscing elit, sed diam nonnumy eiusmod tempor incidunt ut labore et dolore magna aliquam erat volupat.
— Magnus Xeriat

Lorem ipsum dolor sit amet, consectetur adipscing elit, sed diam nonnumy eiusmod tempo incidunt ut labore et dolore.

The Gunning Fog Index is available with some word processing programs. It is not always reliable, however, because computers can't apply common sense and can't allow for exceptions.

Lowering the reading level of your content does not mean "dumbing down" the information. Newsletter writing is chatty, conversational, and informal while still being informative, clear, and to the point. Try reading the material aloud — this allows you to hear the words you're using and gives you the opportunity to adjust the context and tone of your writing. In addition, you'll be able to ensure you're writing in a clear, concise manner without sounding patronizing or condescending.

There are various indices available to gauge whether the reading is difficult or easy. The Gunning Fog Index, a standard in the workplace and used by the Library of Congress, is easy to apply.

There are two variables used in the Gunning Index: the average sentence length and the number of hard words. Difficult words usually have three or more syllables. Adding "ing" or "ed" to a root word, however, does not make it a difficult word. For example, responding is really adding "ing" to respond. In addition, combination words are also not considered difficult words. For example, newsletter is really "news" combined with "letter."

Gunning Fog Index

Average Sentence Length _____

+ Hard Words _____

Total _____

times .4

To simplify language, shorten sentences and substitute easy words for difficult words. Also break compound sentences into two separate sentences. Most of the time, the easiest word is the best word. Why say "numerous" if you mean "many," or "utilize" when you mean "use," or "rehabilitation" when the abbreviation "rehab" can be used just as well?

Knowing your audience is important. For example, if your newsletter is published for a group of professionals in a field such as occupational or physical therapy, they will be familiar with the jargon and technical language of their profession. If the same newsletter is sent to their clients or the families of their clients, however, this language would be difficult for the readers to understand. Because of these distinctions, it is not always wise to rely on computer software, which makes general decisions for a general audience.

Headlines

Headlines are used to grab attention. After reading the headlines, readers determine if they want to read anything else. No matter who's doing the writing, generating headlines is an editorial function. Headlines must be on target. "Topic headlines" just tell the reader what the article is about, but not why they must read on. In order to succeed, a headline must address the "why."

The following technique will help you reliably and predictably generate effective headlines, time after time. Suppose you have written a story about your company's new test lab and assigned a topic headline as a working title. On three separate sheets of paper (or one sheet divided into thirds), make three lists: a list of verbs that relate to your topic, a list of relevant nouns, and a list of the readers you are targeting. On the noun sheet, you may write, "New testing lab"; in the verb section "is open" could be an entry; and "potential customers" might describe the readers you are targeting.

The next task is to come up with a list of synonyms for each word. For "New testing lab," for instance, you may list:

Noun	Reader	Verb
new testing lab	potential customers	is open
innovative facility	client	ready
new building	testers	online
updated lab	end-users	set
state-of-the-art testing lab	buyers	completed
	you	redone
brand spanking new facility	prospects	upgraded
	folks worried about quality	
	integrity-minded consumers	

Excellent headlines share three qualities: They make a specific and direct reference to your readers; they feature an active, involving verb; and they include enough nouns to identify the topic.

- *innovative facility*
- *new building*
- *updated lab*
- *state-of-the-art testing lab*
- *brand-new facility*

and more. You then turn to the reader. Start with "potential customers" and add:

- *clients*
- *testers*
- *end-users*
- *buyers*
- *you*
- *prospects*
- *people worried about quality*
- *integrity-minded consumers*

and the like. Then turn your attention to the verb. You start with "is open" and you add:

- *ready*
- *online*
- *set*
- *completed*
- *redone*
- *upgraded*

and on and on until you run out of ideas.

After you have completed your lists, select one item at a time from each list and play with the combinations until you have created the most effective and "selling" headline possible. In this example, the headline might be:

"State-of-the-Art Lab Ready for Your Quality Checks" or "Customers: Updated Testing Facility Is Online."

Use any method that works for you to write on-target headlines. A headline that works will always grab the readers' eyes and tell them why they should read on.

Leads

A **lead** refers to the first several words or a phrase written to hook the reader's interest. Three styles of lead that work effectively include shared interest, time, and questioning.

The shared interest style immediately grabs readers who share a specific interest. "Music lovers: The company will once again sponsor jazz lunches every Friday all summer," is an example of a lead likely to interest readers fond of music.

"Fly fisherman, like many sportsmen, worry that pollution will endanger ...," "Employees with more than five years service ...," and "WordPerfect users ..." are all examples of the shared-interest style of lead.

The second effective style of lead is to use one or several time-oriented words. Certain words such as "today," "imme-

diately," or "right away" create a sense of urgency. For example, "See Betty in Personnel today about your 401(k) form." Or, "The new interactive software is available now," or "Call immediately for your updated information packet." Since timely and relevant information is the number one favorite of newsletter readers, a sense of urgency in your leads helps your articles get read.

The third idea for leads is to pose a question which the rest of the article answers. Make sure that the question involves the readers and is positive. "Have you ever wondered what a quality checker looks for?" is not as involving a lead as, "Does a quality checker's report impact my job security?" Make the questions positive and personally relevant.

Captions

Put important pieces of information in the **captions**. Captions are read more than body text, so they can be as long as they need to be without losing readers. Do not just identify things in captions, but give the specifics on why the photo, chart, or diagram was chosen to illustrate a point.

A photograph showing a man and woman shaking hands should have a

Empathy Index

Them

Us   <   >

caption that says more than, "Joe Smith and Mary Jones." A better caption would be, "Joe Smith congratulates Mary Jones on winning last quarter's sales awards. Read the article below to see how she did it, and which of her techniques you might be able to implement." Be sure captions speak to the "why" of the photograph or illustration, not merely the "what."

Voice

The term "voice" means several things. First, voice means the tone of the newsletter. The voice of a newsletter should be chatty, relaxed, and conversational.

Second, the term "voice" refers to a proper focus on your reader. The Empathy Index is a way of measuring whether or not the newsletter is outwardly focused. Here's how it works: Take an article and count the number of references to "them" — the reader. Then count the number of references to "us" — the writer or publisher. When you subtract "us" from "them," you should end up with a positive number. References can be by name, by pronoun, or by implication. This index is an effective way of ensuring a proper voice.

The voice becomes much stronger when you focus on your audience. For example, "WE are pleased to announce that OUR new test lab is open and ready for business." In that sentence, we spoke about ourselves twice, and you, our customer, not at all. The next sentence does the opposite: "YOUR test results will be turned around quicker and with greater accuracy, because the new lab is open and ready for YOUR business." When you have a positive Empathy Index, you speak to the customers, not to or about yourself.

When considering the voice, it is helpful to develop a style sheet. A style sheet gives all the grammar, punctuation, and spelling rules your newsletter will use, as well as other pertinent information. Whether you use the Associated Press (AP), Chicago, Gregg Reference, or any other guide, having a comprehensive style sheet will keep your writing consistent and logical, and cut down on editing. The more complete your style sheet, the less editing you'll have to do.

Include decisions about use of titles, capitalization, and punctuation in your style sheet. Also set standards for the use of first name vs. last name, neutral pronouns, and bias-free language.

SECTION THREE, PART ONE: HIGH-IMPACT NEWSLETTER DESIGN

A well-designed newsletter creates a mood, gets attention, and enhances the content. Although newsletters get read primarily because they contain content that readers want to know about, design remains a major factor in attracting specific readers.

In this section, the eight design elements which are the basis of newsletter design will be discussed. Illustrations and examples of a variety of designs are shown, and you'll learn how to gauge your readers' reactions to them. In addition, instructions on how to use clip art and photography to add life and vigor to your newsletter are provided.

Reviewing the terminology of design will help you communicate with designers, printers, your software, and others in the field, and is a logical place to start.

DESIGN TERMINOLOGY

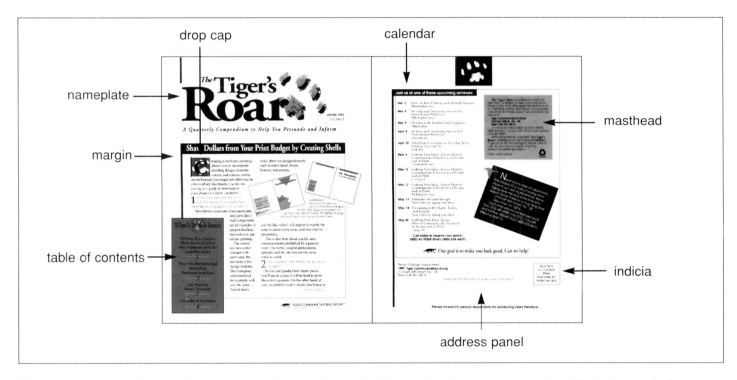

This two-color newsletter targeted middle-level managers who bought marketing services; it was a sales tool, and was very effective.

The margin refers to the outside space between the printed area and the edge of the paper.

The nameplate should not be confused with the masthead. The nameplate is the section that identifies the newsletter. The masthead is a box which gives the reader information about your publication.

The indicia allows you to mail your newsletter. You get it from the post office, and it must fit their specifications exactly.

The table of contents indicates the scope of the newsletter and directs the readers to the content that has the most relevance for them. This section does not have to be called "table of contents" to be effective. "What's In This Issue" or "What's Inside" works just as well. A newsletter editor in Los Angeles has been publishing a one-page, two-sided newsletter for two years, but

when she added a box on the bottom of the first page titled, "What's On the Other Side," readers congratulated her on expanding the newsletter! In this instance, the added table of contents box also served to get more of the newsletter read.

For the newsletter design shown above, a cat's paw was scanned into the system and used as a graphic device. This newsletter was printed two-sided on 11 x 17 paper, so the calendar was on the back.

Inside the two-page spread, the cat's paw at the top of the page helps readers recognize the newsletter. **Clip art** is art, usually line art, which you buy a license to use. When used as shown in this example, positioned to point into the layout, art helps direct the reader's eye. The headline in this illustration is placed in a border.

The empty space across the fold is called the **gutter**. The folio refers to the page number and other information at the bottom of the page.

The space between columns of copy is called the **alley**. (There are three words in newsletter design terminology which refer to empty spaces: the alley between columns of text; the margin on the top, bottom, and sides; and the gutter, over the fold.)

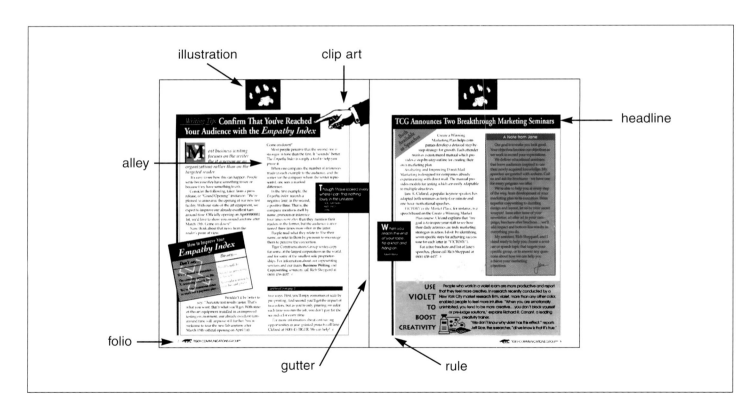

Just as there is no best way to write an article, there is no one best design. The best design decisions, however, are based on readers' preferences.

In this example of six alternative designs, notice the placement of the nameplate, the columnar division of space, and the use of white space. Although all of these designs are professional looking, the one most preferred by readers is Example 1, the one that looks most like a newsletter.

Example 1

The Newsletter News
JUNE 1996
VOLUME 1

Air Quality Newsletter Survives Crisis, Now Enters Third Decade in Bay Area

Example 2

intro line to go here

Do You Know Whom You Are Talking To?

The Newsletter News
VOLUME 1   JUNE 1996

Besides Economy, There Are Reasons to Type Newsletters

THE BARRETT REPORT

Example 3

The Newsletter News
VOLUME 1 • JUNE 1996

intro line to go here

Saucy Newsletter Serves PR, Media People

Example 4

THE NEWSLETTER NEWS
A Publication Of Some Company

VOLUME 1   JUNE 1996

The Interview – A Good Tool To Master

A Subhead Goes Here

Inside:
first article on whatever subject
second feel good article
third article in this newsletter
fourth and final?
yet another article

Example 5

A Subhead Goes Here

New Stylebook Sure to Stir Controversy

– LOOKS LIKE A BYLINE

The Newsletter News
VOLUME 1
JUNE 1996

first article on whatever subject	3
second feel good article	4
third article in this newsletter	5
fourth and final? article	6
yet another article	6

Example 6

A Subhead Goes Here

Forced Humor Defeats Purpose

The Newsletter News
JUNE 1996
VOLUME 1

Leave a Clear Trail For Reader To Follow

first article on whatever subject	1
second feel good article	2
third article newsletter	2
fourth article	3

EIGHT STATIC DESIGN DECISIONS

Match the frequency of your publishing to the quantity of news you have to offer.

The following is a description of eight static design decisions. "Static" means that the design decisions, once made, don't change. With a design that is constant issue after issue, your newsletter can be easily recognized by your readers. This consistency of design and format distinguishes your newsletter from others and helps build a strong image for you and your organization.

1. Size, length, and frequency

The first design decision you need to make concerns the size, length, and frequency of the newsletter. These three variables are usually interrelated. Let's start by reviewing what's being done in newsletters now.

Over 80 percent of all newsletters are 8½ x 11 inches, finished size. They are printed on 11 x 17 paper and folded, or photocopied on letter-size paper and stapled. About ten percent of current newsletters are printed on legal-size paper, which is 8½ by 14; about five percent are tabloids, 11 x 17; and the last five percent are "other." Your newsletter should be 8½ x 11 unless you have a good reason to do something else. The 8½ x 11 newsletter folds into standard-size envelopes and fits in manila folders. It slips into in-baskets at work, fits on top of kitchen counters at home, and is easy to hold and read. It's also the least expensive option, since it is the standard size in business and at home. Be especially careful about selecting a larger size newsletter if your audience is older or physically disabled in any way — it might be hard for them to hold.

Sometimes using a size other than 8½ x 11 helps to achieve a specific

objective. For example, the tourism department of a foreign country sent a newsletter to tour operators in poster form. Each issue featured a stunning photo of an exotic tourist getaway. It was shipped in a poster pack. Since the tourism department's objective was to have clients retain the newsletter, this format was a logical choice.

The majority of newsletters are quarterly; monthly is the next most popular frequency. More frequent publication is less common, but may be appropriate for your newsletter. There is no ideal frequency, just so long as you publish the newsletter on a predictable basis.

In the example at left, you see the 6:30 pm edition of an *hourly* newsletter. Technology is changing two things about newsletters: your readers' expectations and your ability to publish up-to-date information. Publishing an hourly newsletter sounds overwhelming, until you consider that you can set up one template, scan the wire services, electronically position the news stories, and send it via e-mail, fax, or the Internet.

You should consider publishing on the Internet only if you can update your newsletter frequently. Week-old news is as stale on the Internet as anywhere else. If you are publishing on a quarterly basis or if your readers do not have frequent access to the Internet or e-mail, this option is not for you.

Most newsletters are between four and eight pages in length. Longer newsletters are acceptable, but you should keep the length under 36 pages. If a newsletter is longer than 36 pages, it is perceived to be a magazine, journal, or book and, therefore, is much less likely to be read.

If you are having trouble keeping the length under 36 pages, maybe you need to publish more frequently. If, on the other hand, you are having trouble filling a page, you probably need to publish less frequently. If you find it difficult to stay within the page allocation and you can't afford to publish more frequently, you may want to increase the page size from 8½ x 11 to legal size.

The size, length, and frequency of your newsletter are interrelated, so you need to make decisions about these three things at the same time and in relation to one another.

Internet newsletters are becoming more common. CareerTrack's newsletter, "The E-Train," and "Food Stop" offer substantive information. Notice that "Food Stop" starts with a table of contents which guides readers into areas of special interest, such as "Wine & Spirits" with Darrin Siegfried.

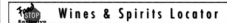

NEWSLETTER
The E-Train

- Articles and excerpts
- Timely training tips
- Subscribe free!
- Training discounts

CareerTrack's
Electronic Training Newsletter

Introducing The E-Train, your ongoing source of personal and professional development information on CareerTrack's World Wide Web site.

The following is a brief preview of what you can expect to see on The E-Train. On a regular basis we'll provide feature stories on relevant training issues as well as brief tips covering a wide range workplace and personal improvement issues.

Here's a sampling of what you'll see in the current issue:

Communicating to Be Liked, Trusted and Respected
by Debra Sutch

Do you ever wonder if there's a quick and easy way to get people to do exactly what you want them to do and get them to like you in the process? Unfortunately, there is no magical formula for getting your way all the time and maintaining strong relationships.

However, good interpersonal communication skills will enable you to clearly ask for what you want in a nonoffensive manner -- even with people you just met.

THE SMALL-TALK AGENDA

Remember the old saying, "Chance favors the prepared mind"? Well, it's particularly true when meeting new people and striking up a conversation. Try preparing an agenda in your mind for engaging in small talk. Simply think of a few topics that you can file in the back of your mind and pull them out for those moments when you're compelled to engage in small talk.

Think of the topics that you know a lot about and can easily discuss. Consider your resources, skills, ideas, experiences, talents, hobbies and passions. Also think about subjects you'd like to learn more about. If you had the chance to ask an expert about any subject, what would you want to learn?

When you have a mental agenda for engaging in small talk, you automatically will have -- and project -- more confidence, enthusiasm and energy.

PULLING YOUR FOOT OUT OF YOUR MOUTH

What happens if you say the wrong thing the first time you meet someone? Here are three things to remember to help you overcome common first-impression blunders:

1. Address the situation quickly. If you stuck your foot in your mouth, it's highly likely the other person noticed. So go ahead and make a comment on it. For example, "Excuse me, Chris, I referred to you as manager. I should have remembered that you were promoted to director."

Nameplate concepts can be adapted to various companies' newsletters. Linked names and the word "link" itself are especially effective. For example, "Faculty Link," "Student Link," and "Parent Link" work well in a school setting. Each newsletter relates to the others, and the names drive home the connection.

2. The nameplate

The nameplate is usually positioned on the top of the front page and is about a quarter of the page in size (about two and a half inches). Ideally, it's immediately recognizable to the reader as yours. The name of the newsletter, the dateline, and the name of the publishing organization should be in the nameplate. You can also include a graphic such as your logo, a subtitle, and color.

The best newsletters have recognizable and original names. If, however, you want to give your newsletter a generic name like "The Bulletin," "The Trumpet," or even "The Newsletter," then be sure to add a subtitle.

The dateline should correspond to your frequency of publication: the name of month if you publish monthly, the season if it's a quarterly, etc. The dateline's format should remain consistent from issue to issue, because a newsletter's success depends on its ability to be recognized, and consistency in design achieves just that.

Even though consistency is the ideal, some newsletters are published only sporadically, whenever there is enough time, money, information, or motivation. The best dateline alternative for this situation is the volume and number

Money Minute$
The ACME Credit Union

December 1996

Join the Credit Union Band

working together to build you a better future!

Lorem ipsum dolor sit amet, consectetuer adipiscing elit, sed d nonummy nibh euismod tincidunt laoreet dolore magna aliquam era volutpat. Ut wisi enim ad minim veniam, quis.Duis autem vel eum iriure dolor in hendrerit in vulputat velit esse molestie consequat, vel illum dolore eu feugiat nulla facilis vero eros et accumsan et iusto od dignissim qui blandit praesent luptatum zzril delenit augue duis dolore te feugait nulla facilisi. Lore ipsum dolor sit amet, consect. Du autem vel eum iriure dolor in hendrerit in vulputate velit esse molestie consequat, vel illum dolo eu feugiat nulla facilisis at vero er et accumsan et iusto odio dignissi qui blandit pr.

Money Matter$
The ACME Credit Union

JANUARY 1996

New Branch Building

Lorem ipsum dolor sit amet, consectetuer adipiscing elit, sed diam nonummy nibh euismod tincidunt ut laoreet dolore magna aliquam erat volutpat. Ut wisi enim ad minim veniam, quis.

Duis autem vel eum iriure dolor in hendrerit in vulputate velit esse molestie consequat, vel illum dolore eu feugiat nulla facilisis at vero eros et accumsan et iusto odio dignissim qui blandit praesent luptatum zzril delenit augue duis dolore te feugait nulla facilisi. Lorem ipsum dolor sit amet, consectetuer.

Duis autem vel eum iriure dolor in hendrerit in vulputate velit esse molestie consequat, vel illum dolore eu feugiat nulla facilisis at vero eros et accumsan et iusto odio dignissim qui blandit praesent luptatum zzril delenit augue duis dolore te feugait nulla facilisi. Lorem ipsum dolor sit amet, consectetuer.

Ut wisi enim ad minim veniam, quis nostrud exerci ut tation ullamcorper suscipit lobortis nisl ut aliquip ex ea.

Also in this Issue...

Lorem ipsum	pg 4
dolor sit amet, nsectetuer	pg 4
adipiscing consequat	pg 2
vel illum dolore	pg 3
eu feugiat	pg 4

IRAs Make Dollars and Sense

Iiriure dolor in hendrerit in vulputate velit esse molestie consequat, vel illum dolore eu feugiat nulla faciliis at vero eros et accumsan et iusto odio dignissim ut qui blandit praesent luptatum zzril delenit te feugait nulla facilisi.

Nam liber tempor cum soluta nobis eleifend option:
- Duis autem vel eum iriure dolor in hendrerit in ut vulputate velit esse molestie consequat uat, vel illum dolore eu feugiat nulla facilisis.

- Lorem ipsum dolor sit amet, consectetuer adipiscing elit, sed diam nonummy nibh euismod tincidunt ut laoreet dolore magna aliquam erat volutpat. Ut wisi enim ad minim veniam, quis nostrud exerci ut tation ullamcorper lobortis nisl ut commodo consequat.

Nam liber tempor cum soluta nobis eleifend option:
- Duis autem vel eum iriure dolor in hendrerit in ut vulputate velit esse uat, eu feugiat nulla facilisis.

- Lorem ipsum dolor sit amet, consectetuer adipiscing elit, sed diam nonummy nibh euismod tincidunt ut laoreet dolore magna aliquam erat volutpat. Ut.

Nam liber tempor cum soluta nobis eleifend option Duis autem vel eum iriure dolor in hendrerit in vulputate velit esse molestie consequat, Ut wisi Lorem:
- Duis autem vel eum iriure dolor in hendrerit in ut vulputate velit esse molestie consequat uat, vel illum dolore eu feugiat nulla facilisis.

- Lorem ipsum dolor sit amet, consectetuer adipiscing elit, sed diam nonummy nibh euismod tincidunt ut laoreet dolore magna aliquam erat volutpat.

Duis autem vel eum iriure dolor in hendrerit in vulputate velit esse molestie consequat. s at vero eros et accumsan et iusto odio dignissim ut qui blandit praesent luptatum zzril delenit te feugait nulla facilisi

Start a Payroll Deduction Plan Today!

Lorem ipsum dolor sit amet, consectetuer adipiscing elit, sed diam nonummy nibh euismod tincidunt ut laoreet dolore magna aliquam erat volutpat. Ut wisi enim ad minim veniam, quis.

Duis autem vel eum iriure dolor in hendrerit in vulputate velit esse molestie consequat, vel illum dolore eu feugiat nulla facilisis at vero eros et accumsan et iusto odio dignissim

qui blandit praesent luptatum zzril delenit augue duis dolore te feugait nulla facilisi. Lorem ipsum dolor sit amet, consectetuer.

Duis autem vel eum iriure dolor in hendrerit in vulputate velit esse molestie consequat, vel illum dolore eu feugiat nulla facilisis at vero eros et accumsan et iusto odio dignissim qui blandit praesent luptatum zzril delenit augue duis dolore.

convention. If the newsletter's dateline is Vol. III, No. 8, for example, it tells the reader that you have been publishing the newsletter for three years and that this is the eighth issue in the current year. Newsletters datelined this way stay "fresh" and are likely to be kept longer because there is no month, quarter, or season to remind the reader of the publication date.

Look at the example on the left. When you see the title, "Money Matter$," it is clear that the publisher is an investment house, bank, credit union, or some other financial institution. The name of the newsletter connects it with the publishing organization. Sometimes this publisher has news that can't wait until the next regularly published newsletter, and they meet that challenge by publishing "Money Minute$," a name that immediately relates to the original.

Can you see how they relate? Both publications feature the same nameplate font in the same size, boldness, and position. The vertical line through the ending "S" provides a cohesive connection.

Money Minute$ readers know immediately who's publishing it, and that it contains more timely information than Money Matter$. The use of connected names helps readers to feel part of the group, always a plus for a newsletter publisher.

Now look at the example to the right. It's another company's newsletter that uses the same name. Because names aren't copyrightable, and because the title is handled in a very different way by each publisher, many organizations can use the same name and it will be effective for each.

MONEY MATTER$

Winter 1995

Main Street Booking Service

IN THIS ISSUE
- *Lorem ipsum dolor*
- *sit amet, consectetuer*
- *adipiscing elit, sed*
- *diam nonummy nibh euismod tincidunt ut laor*
- *dolore magna aliquam*
- *erat volutpat. Ut wisi enim a minim veniam, quis nostrud*
- *exerci tation ullamcorper*
- *suscipit lobortis nisl*

Lorem ipsum dolor sit amet
Lorem ipsum dolor
sit amet, consectetuer
adipiscing elit, sed

diam nonummy nibh euismod
tincidunt ut laor
dolore magna aliquam
erat volu
m veniam, quis nostrud exerci
tation ullamcorper

suscipit lobortis nisl
ut aliquip ex ea
commodo consequat.
Duis autem vel eum iriure
dolor in hendrerit i

n vulputate velit esse
molestie consequat

Visit The Car Dealership ARMED ... With The FACTS!

I facilisi. Lorem ipsum dolor sit amet, con se etuer adipiscing elit, sed diam nonummy nibh euismod tincidunt ut lao reet dolore magnaaliquam erat volutpat. Ut wisi enim ad minim veniam, quis nostrud exerci ut tation ullamcorper Duis autem vel eum iriure dolor in hendrerit in vulputate velit esse molestie consequat, vel illum dolore eu feugiat nulla facilisis at vero eros et accumsan et iusto odio dignissim ut qui blandit praesent luptatum zzril delenit augue duis dolore te feugait nulla facilisi.

Nam liber tempor cum soluta nobis eleifend option congue nihil imperdiet doming id quod wisi enim ad minim veniam, quis nostrud exerci ut tation ullamcorper suscipit lobortis nisl ut aliquip ex ea commodo consequat.

Duis autem vel eum iriure dolor in hendrerit in ut vulputate velit esse molestie consequat uat, vel illum dolore eu feugiat nulla facilisis.

LIQUID Stocks!

Y facilisi. Lorem ipsum dolor sit amet, consectetuer adipiscing elit, sed diam nonummy nibh euismod tincidunt ut laoreet dolore magna aliquam erat volutpat. Ut wisi enim ad minim veniam, quis nostrudexerci ut in hendrerit in vulputate velit esse molestie consequat, vel iusto odio dignissim ut qui blandit praesent luptatum zzril delenit augue duis dolore te feugait nulla facilisi. **dolore magna aliquam erat volutpat**

LOW **8.5%** APR
Borrow up to 75% of the stock's value

Nam liber tempor cum soluta nobis eleifend option congue nihil imperdiet doming id quod wisi enim ad minim veniam, quis nostrud nisl ut aliquip ex ea commodo consequat.

Here's another idea you may be able to use. The concept here is to select silhouettes which represent your audience. The art signals to the readers that the newsletter is targeting them.

"Spectrum," a newsletter published by the Greenwich, Connecticut, public schools, does a lovely job of illustrating their readers. Notice the silhouettes of children in various positions. Specifically, note the balance of boys and girls, kids sitting and active, and children of various ages involved in different activities. Also note that the figure on the far right is kicking the ball *into* the layout, not off the page. The nameplate is so distinctive, it will build a strong identity for the newsletter right away.

"Puddles" does the same thing. By using appealing, distinctive silhouettes of characters in a variety of active poses, the nameplate achieves a dis-

tinctive, compelling look. Notice how rain is suggested through angled lines, and motion is suggested through horizontal lines.

SPECTRUM

Spring 1991   A Look Across the Greenwich Public Schools   No. 6

1990-1991:
The Year of the Arts

Can you imagine a world without the arts? They pervade almost every aspect of our lives. They play a role in our leisure time, in our religions, our social life, our businesses, and our government.

We hear music everywhere — on our radios, and on our televisions, at concerts, in stores and restaurants. We enjoy paintings on our walls at home and in our art galleries. The furniture we use, our houses, our cars, our clothes and fabrics have been designed by artists, and each time you turn on the television, or go to a play or listen to the radio, you're exposed to acting, writing, and music.

Who provides the many sounds of music, the paint strokes on a picture, or the acting in the plays you see? Yesterday's students! Who will design tomorrow's buildings and cars, provide us with new creative ideas in business, compose and sing new songs, entertain us with future drama productions? The responsibility will lie with today's students, and they will be able to meet the challenge only if they are given the opportunities to develop the necessary artistic talents. Recognizing this important role that the arts play, State Commissioner of Education Gerald Tirozzi has proclaimed 1991 "The Year of the Arts in Education."

GHS music students participated in the All-State music competition at the University of Connecticut at Storrs in May. These students represent the best of the music department having gone through two auditions and the Western Regionals to be accepted at All-State. In the back row, from the left, are David Hughes (trumpet, jazz band), and Task Toyono (violin, orchestra). In the front, from the right, are Maureen Hughes (violin, orchestra), Nam Tran (violin, orchestra) and Ellen Ebright (voice, chorus).

puddles

A Publication Of Some Company   VOLUME II · MARCH 1996

When it RAINS it pours
A Subhead Goes Here

Lorem ipsum dolor sit amet, consectetuer adipiscing elit, sed diam nonummy nibh euismod tincidunt ut laoreet dolore magna aliquam erat volutpat. Ut wisi enim ad minim veniam, quis nostrud exerci tation ullamcorper suscipit lobortis nisl ut aliquip ex ea commodo consequat.

Duis autem vel eum iriure dolor in hendrerit in vulputate velit esse molestie consequat, vel illum dolore eu feugiat nulla facilisis at vero eros et accumsan et iusto odio dignissim qui blandit praesent luptatum zzril delenit augue duis dolore te feugait nulla facilisi. Lorem ipsum dolor sit amet, consectetuer adipiscing elit, sed diam nonummy nibh euismod tincidunt ut laoreet dolore magna aliquam erat volutpat.

Ut wisi enim ad minim veniam, quis nostrud exerci tation ullamcorper suscipit lobortis nisl ut aliquip ex ea commodo consequat. Duis autem vel eum iriure dolor in hendrerit in vulputate velit esse molestie consequat, vel illum dolore eu feugiat nulla facilisis at vero eros et accumsan et iusto odio dignissim qui blandit praesent luptatum zzril delenit augue duis dolore te feugait nulla facilisi.

Nam liber tempor cum soluta nobis eleifend option congue nihil imperdiet doming id quod mazim placerat facer possim assum. Lorem ipsum dolor sit amet, consectetuer adipiscing elit, sed diam nonummy nibh euismod tincidunt ut laoreet dolore magna aliquam erat volutpat.

Ut wisi enim ad minim veniam, quis nostrud exerci tation ullamcorper suscipit lobortis nisl ut aliquip ex ea commodo consequat.

Duis autem vel eum iriure dolor in hendrerit in vulputate velit esse molestie consequat, vel illum dolore eu feugiat nulla facilisis.

Lorem ipsum dolor sit amet, consectetuer adipiscing elit, sed diam nonummy nibh euismod tincidunt ut laoreet dolore magna aliquam erat volutpat. Ut wisi enim ad minim veniam, quis nostrud exerci tation ullamcorper suscipit lobortis nisl ut aliquip ex ea commodo consequat.

Duis autem vel eum iriure dolor in hendrerit in vulputate velit esse molestie consequat, vel illum dolore eu feugiat nulla facilisi. Lorem ipsum dolor sit amet, consectetuer adipiscing elit, sed diam nonummy nibh euismod tincidunt ut laoreet dolore magna aliquam erat volutpat.

Ut wisi enim ad minim veniam, quis nostrud exerci tation ullamcorper suscipit lobortis nisl ut aliquip ex ea commodo consequat. Duis autem vel eum iriure dolor in hendrerit in vulputate velit esse molestie consequat, vel illum dolore eu feugiat nulla facilisis at vero eros et accumsan et iusto odio dignissim qui blandit praesent luptatum zzril delenit augue duis dolore te feugait nulla facilisi.

Nam liber tempor cum soluta nobis eleifend option congue nihil imperdiet doming id quod ma zim placerat facer possim assum. Lorem ipsum dolor sit amet, consectetuer adipiscing elit, sed diam nonummy nibh euismod tincidunt ut laoreet dolore magna aliquam erat volutpat.

Ut wisi enim ad minim veniam, quis nostrud exerci tation ullamcorper suscipit lobortis nisl ut aliquip ex ea commodo consequat.

Duis autem vel eum iriure dolor in hendrerit in vulputate velit esse molestie consequat, vel illum dolore eu feugiat nulla facilisis.

	e nihil imperdiet do
Inside:	
first article on whatever subject	1
second feel good article	2
third article in this newsletter	2
fourth and final? article	3
yet another article	4

The Washington State Department of Social & Health Services' newsletter, "The Network News," expands on this concept. They take silhouettes representing members of their community and replicate them to form a dramatic border. Note that the silhouettes appear to be holding hands and walking forward. The half-people that appear on both the left and right edges suggest that the line of marching citizens continues indefinitely.

CareerTrack also uses a silhouette in its trainer newsletter. Note that as a customer-focused company, CareerTrack wisely includes several seminar attendees in the silhouette.

THE NETWORK NEWS

Washington State Department of Social and Health Services
Mental Health Division, Carrol Hernandez, Director

AUTUMN 1994

Work Group Examines N...
Comprehensive Crisis Re...

"I think there is a real need in this state for a comprehensive system that serves all people who experience a crisis," asserts Pete Blair, Mental Health Division (MHD) program administrator.

Blair has been involved since the first of this year with a Comprehensive Crisis Response System (CCRS) work group, which has included representatives from each of the Divisions in the Department of Social and Health Services.

What Blair envisions is a crisis response system which employs a cross-system team approach that goes out and stays with someone in crisis until the situation is resolved.

"Often what occurs now is that someone in the mental health crisis response system goes out, but if he or she determines that it is not a mental health crisis, then the person needing help is referred to another system," he says. "This means that someone from another system must come in and repeat the determination to ascertain if the crisis is appropriate for that system."

Blair suggests that this creates gaps in service, where an individual in crisis may not get served at all, or the repeated need to determine which is the appropriate system to serve the consumer, causes a duplication of services. In the meantime, the person needing help may become more acute and have to be hospitalized when, perhaps, the situation could have been resolved earlier without hospitalization.

Ray Antonsen, Region 1 Division of Alcohol and Sub... member of the CCRS work and feels that an ideal comp... system would be comprised... mental health, alcohol and ... mental disabilities, aging a... families fields.

"Such a system needs to ... needs of the community—o... comments.

He indicates that one co... of mental health and substa... who go out and make a det... person's behavior and then... with a referral to a case ma... team might bring the perso... observation.

"A comprehensive crisis ... lot of different shapes," An... goal would be to keep indi... the cracks and prevent inap... by seeing people in the fiel... ate referrals based on their...

"Whatever shape it take... case management compone... utilizers, to minimize repea... Mary Sarno, MHD prog... member of the CCRS work ... team approach is essential ...

Please turn to Page 3

INSIDE

How It's Working ....
Professional Comment...
Family Advocate New...

Pete Blair, MHD program administra...

Ray Antonsen, Region 1 administra... tor, Division of Alcohol and Substance Abuse

Mary Sarno, MHD program administra... tor

The

CareerTrainer

December 1995

IN THIS ISSUE
Page 1... **3Q95 Trainer Awards** *by Diane Montgomery*
Page 3... **How to Be All Things to All Attendees** *by Christie Ward*
Page 4... **A Favorite Exercise** *by Lani Arredondo*

ACKNOWLEDGMENTS
Compilation and Layout:
Kristen Goldner

Editors:
Diane Montgomery
Patricia LeChevalier

3Q95 Trainer Quarterly Awards
by Diane Montgomery

Most Outstanding Testimonial
Susan Freeman

Lorem ipsum dolor sit amet, consectetur adipscing elit, sed diam nonnumy eiusmod tempor incidunt ut labore et dolore magna aliquam erat volupat. Ut enim ad minimim veniami quis nostnud exercitation ullamcorpor suscipit laboris nisi ut aliquip ex ea commodo consequat. Duis autem vel eum irure dolor in repre-henderit in voluptate velit esse molestaie son consequat, vel illum dolore eu hic tenetury sapiente delectus au aut prefer asp riore rquam erat v nlupa minimim veniami quis nostrud exerc land praesent aigue duos dolor et molestais excceptur sint occae-cal prnvident simil tem or sunt in cula nui.

Sales Superstar
Cherie Cross

Ut enim ad minimim veniami quis nostnud exercitation ullam-corpor suscipit laboris nisi ut aliquip ex ea commodo consequat. Duis autem vel eum irure dolor in reprehenderit in voluptate velit esse molestaie son consequat, vel illum dolore eu hic tenetury sapiente delectus iore rquam erat v nlupa minimim suscipit laboris nisi ut aliquip ex ea commodoveniami quis nostrud exerc land praesent aigue duos dolor et molestais excceptur sint occae-cal prnvident simil tem or sunt in cula nui.

Notice that the silhouettes are shown in motion: walking or gesturing. Implied action adds interest.

A good cost-saving strategy is the newsletter **shell**. A shell consists of the elements of the newsletter that are the same in every issue, preprinted on your publication's paper. For each issue, type the contents in your word-processor and photocopy (or print) on this paper. Keep in mind you shouldn't preprint more than about a year's supply, as paper is perishable.

The name "Templine" obviously keys to the organization's industry. The subtitle "Confidential Brief for Health Care Professionals" further narrows their market segment. As soon as you see the nameplate, you know exactly what kind of business this company is in, and that's the mark of a good newsletter.

The format lends itself to short, useful sections of content generated via word processing, which makes this a great example of an extremely low cost newsletter that provides the publisher a great deal of flexibility.

In each issue, the text is laid out in the wider column. With the narrow left column blank, the layout is in balance. The darker illustration — the photo — positioned in an unusual shape in the bottom right corner would overpower the layout if not for the large screened area.

*Temp***LINE** CONFIDENTIAL BRIEF FOR HEALTH CARE PROFESSIONALS

MJ Care, Inc.
Corporate West
350 Bishops Way Suite 230
Brookfield, WI 53005
800 • 877 • 7018

Sandy Nyffeler
Vice President,
Professional Placement

Sandy's Insight

Right away, it's clear that the company which publishes "The Daily Scoop" has something to do with ice cream. Notice the dateline: "Latest edition." This is a clever way to avoid rendering their newsletter out of date. When they print a new issue, it too is called the "latest edition." Thus whenever someone picks it up it looks fresh and timely. Obviously this will only work if the newsletter's content isn't perishable, but if it has a reasonably long shelf life, this can be an effective strategy to prolong a newsletters' usefulness.

These promotional newsletters both offer detailed information that is of interest to their targeted readers. Also note that in "Presidents Vice Presidents Only," the chart is sized to catch readers' eyes. In "The Daily Scoop," the art is large and dramatically colored.

THE DAILY SCOOP

LATEST EDITION

EXTRA, EXTRA!

Read All About It ...

Crowd Goes Wild for Delicious Desserts Served Daily ...

Lorem ipsum dolor sit amet, consectetuer adipiscing elit, sed diam nonummy nibh euismod tincidunt ut laoreet dolore magna aliquam erat volutpat. Ut wisi enim ad minim veniam, quis nostrud exerci tation ullamcorper suscipit lobortis nisl ut aliquip ex ea commodo consequat. Duis autem vel eum iriure dolor in hendrerit in vulputate velit esse molestie consequat, vel illum dolore eu feugiat nulla

Manager Calls News Conference ...

New Better Tasting Ice Cream and Fresh Bakery Items

Mor in hendrerit in vulputate velit esse molestie consequat, Ut wisi Lorem ipsum dolor sit amet, consectetuer adipiscing elit, sed diam nonummy nibh euismod nostrud exerci ut tation ullamcorper suscipit lobortis nisl ut aliquip ex ea commodo consequat.

Enim ad minim veniam, quis nostrud exerci ut tation ullamcorper suscipit lobortis nisl ut aliquip ex ea commodo

Lorem ipsum dolor sit amet, consectetuer adipiscing elit, sed diam nonummy nibh euismod tincidunt ut laoreet dolore magna aliquam erat volutpat. Ut wisi enim ad minim veniam, quis nostrud exerci tation ullamcorper suscipit lobortis

velit esse molestie consequat, Ut wisi Lorem ipsum dolor sit amet, consectetuer adipiscing elit, sed diam nonummy nibh euismod nostrud exerci ut tation ullamcorper suscipit lobortis nisl ut aliquip ex ea commodo consequat.

Enim ad minim veniam, quis nostrud exerci ut tation ullamcorper suscipit lobortis nisl ut aliquip ex ea commodo

PRESIDENTS VICE PRESIDENTS ONLY

DAVID WERNER *International*

Executive Marketplace Trends by David Werner

Although it is clear new job generation has been impressive in the last year or two, the vast majority of these new jobs is low-paying and in no way can be classified middle or upper management.

The second hard fact—and this is encouraging—is that there have been clear indications that companies are, more than ever, emphasizing affirmative action hiring policies.

The third fact is that the restructuring of "corporate America" (and there are many names given to this process) is a continuing process: we all know of companies that have been "restructured" at least twice in the past two or three years.

A fourth fact (according to some senior executive clients who have interviewed with retained recruiters) is that executives "in transition" are not as "desirable" as those currently employed: "Our client," says the

recruiter, "would prefer someone already in place ... and who can be seduced away."

Finally, interim management recruiters are very busy and more and more companies prefer to employ prospects on a specific project-by-project basis. Many of these interim management assignments are converted to full-time positions. This, incidentally, is probably healthy for both parties.

What are the employment trends for 1995? Frankly, more of the same. Clearly, Wall Street is under pressure, perhaps also banking and insurance. General Managers who don't have a specific technology or market niche to offer will find it difficult.

Bright spots? international, Europe, Asia ... within the services sectors (telecommunications, software, travel, entertainment, hospitality, etc.).

The Werner Economic Opportunity Index rates executive opportunity in comparison to a standard set in 1987 for placement ads run in the Eastern edition of the *Wall Street Journal*. Current ad lineage is now half of what it was for the comparable period in 1987.

The Index shows the effect of corporate America's effort at downsizing on management employment opportunities.

Here's a powerful way to connect with your target readers: Name the newsletter after them. If the entire purpose of your newsletter can be summed up by focusing on your readers, this may well be an approach you want to adopt. This executive placement company targets only a few business people, very senior level executives, and so it named the newsletter after them.

Consider running a contest for your newsletter's name. If you decide to do so, make it clear that entrants don't have to be artists, that you're looking for a concept, not a finished version of the nameplate.

Some editors have reported great success with contests. Your results will depend on the level of commitment in your organization, its size, and how you position your request.

However, when dealing with sensitive issues, such as managing major emergencies, plastic surgery, or weight loss, for example, consider skipping the contest, and don't try to be too clever. Instead, select a more innocuous name.

The next two examples illustrate where a generic title – such as "The Newsletter," "The Bulletin," or "The Trumpet" – might have been a better choice. The example at right is based on a newsletter actually published by a major city's emergency workers (the firefighters, emergency medical technicians, and ambulance drivers). Do you see the problem?

Popular Catastrophe

A Monthy Report on Managing Major Emergencies

ANOTHER NEWSLETTER?

NOTE FROM THE DIRECTOR
W.Steve Collier

Lorem ipsum dolor sit amet, consectetuer adipiscing elit, sed diam nonummy nibh euismod tincidunt ut laoreet dolore magna aliquam erat volutpat. Ut wisi enim ad minim veniam, quis nostrud exerci tation ullamcorper suscipit lobortis nisl ut aliquip ex ea commodo consequat.

Duis autem vel eum iriure dolor in hendrerit in vulputate velit esse molestie consequat, vel illum dolore eu feugiat nulla facilisis at vero eros et accumsan et iusto odio dignissim qui blandit praesent luptatum zzril delenit augue duis dolore te feugait nulla facilisi. Lorem ipsum dolor sit amet, consectetuer adipiscing elit, sed diam nonummy nibh euismod tincidunt ut laoreet dolore magna aliquam erat volutpat.

Ut wisi enim ad minim veniam, quis nostrud exerci ut tation ullamcorper suscipit lobortis nisl ut aliquip ex ea commodo consequat. Duis autem vel eum iriure dolor in hendrerit in vulputate velit esse molestie consequat, vel illum dolore eu feugiat nulla facilisis at vero eros et accumsan et iusto odio dignissim ut qui blandit praesent luptatum zzril delenit augue duis dolore te feugait nulla facilisi.

Nam liber tempor cum soluta nobis eleifend option congue nihil imperdiet doming id quod wisi enim ad minim veniam, quis nostrud exerci ut tation ullamcorper suscipit lobortis nisl ut aliquip ex ea commodo consequat.

Duis autem vel eum iriure dolor in hendrerit in ut vulputate velit esse molestie consequat uat, vel illum dolore eu feugiat nulla facilisis.

Lorem ipsum dolor sit amet, consectetuer adipiscing elit, sed diam nonummy nibh euismod tincidunt ut laoreet dolore magna aliquam erat

volutpat. Ut wisi enim ad minim veniam, quis nostrud exerci ut tation ullamcorper suscipit lobortis nisl ut aliquip ex ea commodo consequat.

Duis autem vel eum iriure dolor in hendrerit in ut vulputate velit esse molestie consequat uat, vel illum dolore eu feugiat nulla facilisis.

Duis autem vel eum iriure dolor in hendrerit in vulputate velit esse molestie consequat, Ut wisi Lorem ipsum dolor sit amet, consectetuer adipiscing elit, sed diam nonummy nibh euismod tincidunt ut laoreet dolore magna aliquam erat volutpat. Ut wisi enim ad minim veniam, quis nostrud exerci tation ullamcorper suscipit lobortis nisl ut aliquip ex ea commodo consequat.

Duis autem vel eum iriure dolor in hendrerit in vulputate velit esse molestie consequat, vel illum dolore eu feugiat nulla facilisis at vero eros et accumsan et iusto odio dignissim qui blandit praesent luptatum zzril delenit augue duis dolore te feugait nulla facilisi. Lorem ipsum dolor sit amet, consectetuer adipiscing elit, sed diam nonummy nibh euismod tincidunt ut laoreet dolore magna aliquam erat volutpat.

Ut wisi enim ad minim veniam, quis nostrud exerci ut tation ullamcorper suscipit lobortis nisl ut aliquip ex ea commodo consequat.

EMERGENCY MANAGEMENT — A COMMUNITY EFFORT

Pete Brewster

sectetuer adipiscing elit, sed diam nonummy nibh euismod tincidunt ut laoreet dolore magna aliquam erat volutpat. Ut wisi enim ad minim veniam, quis nostrud exerci tation ullamcorper suscipit lobortis nisl ut aliquip ex ea commodo consequat.

Duis autem vel eum iriure dolor in hendrerit in vulputate velit esse molestie consequat, vel illum dolore eu feugiat nulla facilisis at vero eros et accumsan et iusto odio dignissim qui blandit praesent luptatum zzril delenit augue duis dolore te feugait nulla facilisi. Lorem ipsum dolor sit amet, consectetuer adipiscing elit, sed diam nonummy nibh euismod tincidunt ut laoreet dolore magna aliquam erat volutpat.

Ut wisi enim ad minim veniam, quis nostrud exerci ut tation ullamcorper suscipit lobortis nisl ut aliquip ex ea commodo consequat. Duis autem vel eum iriure dolor in hendrerit in vulputate velit esse molestie consequat, vel illum dolore

continued on page 3

In This Issue

hair talk

A QUARTERLY UPDATE FOR CLIENTS OF HAIR REPLACEMENT

Fall 1996

LOREM IPSUM DOLOR SIT AMET CONSECTETUER ADIPISCING
by some doctor, M.D.

Lorem ipsum dolor sit amet, consectetuer adipiscing elit, sed diam nonummy nibh euismod tincidunt ut laoreet dolore magna aliquam erat volutpat. Ut wisi enim ad minim veniam, quis nostrud exerci tation ullamcorper suscipit lobortis nisl ut aliquip ex ea commodo consequat. Lorem ipsum dolor sit amet, consectetuer adipiscing elit, sed diam nonummy nibh euismod tincidunt ut laoreet dolore magna aliquam erat volutpat. Ut wisi enim ad minim veniam, quis nostrud exerci tation ullamcorper suscipit lobortis nisl ut aliquip ex ea commodo consequat.

Duis autem vel eum iriure dolor in hendrerit in vulputate velit esse molestie consequat, vel illum dolore eu feugiat nulla facilisis at vero eros et accumsan et iusto odio dignissim qui blandit praesent luptatum zzril delenit augue duis dolore te feugait nulla facilisi. Lorem ipsum dolor sit amet, consectetuer adipiscing elit, sed diam nonummy nibh euismod tincidunt ut laoreet dolore magna aliquam erat volutpat.

Ut wisi enim ad minim veniam, quis nostrud exerci ut tation ullamcorper suscipit lobortis nisl ut aliquip ex ea commodo consequat. Duis autem vel eum iriure dolor in hendrerit in vulputate velit esse molestie consequat, vel illum dolore eu feugiat nulla facilisis at vero eros et accumsan et iusto odio dignissim ut qui blandit praesent luptatum zzril delenit augue duis dolore te feugait nulla facilisi.

Nam liber tempor cum soluta nobis eleifend option congue nihil imperdiet doming id quod wisi enim ad minim veniam, quis nostrud exerci ut tation ullamcorper suscipit lobortis nisl ut aliquip ex ea commodo consequat.

Duis autem vel eum iriure dolor in hendrerit in ut vulputate velit esse molestie consequat uat, vel illum dolore eu feugiat nulla facilisis.

Lorem ipsum dolor sit amet, consectetuer adipiscing elit, sed diam nonummy nibh euismod tincidunt ut laoreet dolore magna aliquam erat

Lorem ipsum dolor sit, consectetuer adipiscing nonummy elit, sed diam nibh euismod tincid unt ut laoreet dolore

LOREM IPSUM DOLOR SIT AMET CONSECTETUER ADIPISCING
by some doctor, M.D.

• Lorem ipsum dolor sit amet, consectetuer adipiscing elit, sed diam nonummy nibh

• euismod tincidunt ut laoreet dolore

• magna aliquam erat volutpat. Ut wisi enim

• ad minim veniam, quis nostrud exerci tation ullamcorper suscipit

lobortis nisl ut aliquip ex ea commodo consequat. Lorem ipsum dolor sit amet, consectetuer adipiscing elit, sed diam nonummy nibh euismod tincidunt ut laoreet dolore magna aliquam erat volutpat.

Lorem ipsum dol sit, consetue as u picing noummy elit, sediam nibh ismod tini dunt ut laoreet dolore

Ut wisi enim ad minim veniam, quis nostrud exerci tation ullamcorper suscipit lobortis nisl ut aliquip ex ea commodo consequat.Duis autem vel eum iriure dolor in hendrerit in vulputate velit esse molestie consequat, vel illum dolore eu feugiat nulla facilisis at vero eros et accumsan et iusto odio dignissim qui blandit praesent luptatum zzril delenit augue duis dolore te feugait nulla facilisi.

Lorem ipsum dolor sit amet, consectetuer adipiscing elit, sed diam nonummy nibh euismod tincidunt ut laoreet dolore magna aliquam erat volutpat. Ut wisi enim ad minim veniam, quis nostrud exerci ut tation ullamcorper suscipit lobortis nisl ut aliquip ex ea commodo consequat. Duis autem vel eum iriure dolor in hendrerit in vulputate velit esse molestie consequat, vel illum dolore eu feugiat nulla facilisis at vero eros et accumsan et iusto odio dignissim ut qui blandit praesent luptatum zzril delenit augue duis dolore te feugait nulla facilisi.

Nam liber tempor cum soluta nobis eleifend option congue nihil imperdiet doming id quod wisi enim ad minim veniam, quis nostrud exerci ut tation ullamcorper suscipit lobortis nisl ut aliquip ex ea commodo consequat.

Duis autem vel eum iriure dolor in hendrerit in ut vulputate velit esse molestie consequat uat, vel illum dolore eu feugiat nulla facilisis.Lorem ipsum dolor sit amet, consectetuer adipiscing elit, sed diam nonummy nibh euismod tincidunt ut laoreet dolore magna aliquam erat

This example demonstrates the same problem. This newsletter is targeting an audience about a sensitive issue. People who have had hair replacement surgery probably don't want the letter carrier or their neighbors to know about it.

There's no reason to select a highly descriptive name when targeting a highly interested audience. Recipients of hair replacement therapy, for example, have shown a commitment to the subject that would lead most editors to infer that they'll happily read quarterly updates; they don't need the same boost as, say, the 30,000 employees of a highly decentralized and diverse multinational corporation.

Consider your readers' attitudes toward you as well as your objectives for the newsletter. Most of the time, it's appropriate to select a name that describes your organization, your audience, or your cause. Once the name is selected and a harmonious design created, invite people in and let them get to know you.

Avoid names that some — but not all — of your audience will recognize. If they don't understand, at a glance, who you are, they're likely to conclude that you're not for them.

Without a masthead, some readers may wonder "who really is publishing this thing?"

3. The masthead

It is important that every newsletter have a masthead, because it lets the readers know who publishes the newsletter and how to get in touch with them should they want to.

There are six pieces of information which should be in the masthead: the name and mailing address of the publisher (including postal codes, phone numbers, e-mail, and Internet information, as appropriate); your name and title; a list of the members of the Editorial Advisory Board and any contributing editors; copyright and reprint information; subscription information (or information on how to get on or off the mailing list); and any necessary disclaimers. For example, a stock or investment newsletter's disclaimer might inform readers that a stock's past history does not indicate its future performance.

The masthead at right was adapted from the Coast Guard. Notice how it says, "Printed monthly for Ali Bakian and all the men and women of the Acme Widget Company." The next month it said, "Printed monthly for Jenny Davis and all the men and women of the Acme Widget Company." How about collecting photos of your members, or your employees, or whomever it is you're targeting? This is an excellent way of personalizing the newsletter for its readers. Notice that both examples have the masthead positioned in the same place. It doesn't matter where, just so long as it's static.

List in the masthead all the information that readers need in order to get in touch with you. The woman who published a newsletter for her nursing home had a masthead that read: "Out on Mondays by noon, or come to Room 17." Whether it's simple or complex in design and content, always include a masthead in your newsletter.

2 Acme News   November 1996

In brief...

Lorem ipsum dolor sit consectetuer

Lorem ipsum dolor sit amet, consectetuer adipiscing elit, sed diam nonummy nibh euismod tincidunt ut laoreet dolore magna aliquam erat volutpat. Ut wisi enim ad minim veniam, quis nostrud exerci tation ullamcorper suscipit lobortis nisl ut aliquip ex ea commodo consequat.

Duis autem vel eum iriure dolor in hendrerit in vulputate velit esse molestie consequat, vel illum dolore eu feugiat nulla facilisis at vero eros et accumsan et iusto odio dignissim qui blandit praesent luptatum zzril delenit augue duis dolore te feugait nulla facilisi. Lorem ipsum dolor sit amet, consectetuer adipiscing elit, sed diam nonummy nibh euismod tincidunt ut laoreet dolore magna aliquam erat volutpat.

Lorem ipsum dolor sit amet, consectetuer

Duis autem vel eum iriure dolor in hendrerit in ut vulputate velit esse molestie consequat uat, vel illum dolore eu feugiat nulla facilisi. Lorem ipsum dolor sit amet, consectetuer adipiscing elit, sed diam nonummy nibh euismod tincidunt ut laoreet dolore magna aliquam erat volutpat. Ut wisi enim ad minim veniam, quis nostrud exerci tation ullamcorper suscipit lobortis nisl ut aliquip ex ea commodo consequat.

Duis autem vel eum iriure dolor in hendrerit in vulputate velit esse molestie consequat, Ut wisi Lorem ipsum dolor sit amet, consectetuer adipiscing elit, sed

diam nonummy nibh euismod nostrud exerci ut tation ullamcorper suscipit lobortis nisl ut aliquip ex ea commodo consequat.

Ut wisi enim ad minim veniam, quis nostrud exerci ut tation ullamcorper suscipit lobortis nisl ut aliquip ex ea commodo consequat. Duis autem vel eum iriure dolor in hendrerit in vulputate velit esse molestie consequat, vel illum dolore eu feugiat nulla facilisis at vero eros et accumsan et iusto odio dignissim ut qui blandit praesent luptatum zzril delenit augue duis dolore te feugait nulla facilisi.

Nam liber tempor cum soluta nobis eleifend option congue nihil imperdiet doming id quod wisi enim ad minim veniam, quis nostrud exerci ut tation ullamcorper suscipit lobortis nisl ut aliquip ex ea commodo consequat.

Lorem ipsum dolor sit amet, consectetuer

Duis autem vel eum iriure dolor in hendrerit in vulputate velit esse molestie consequat, vel illum dolore eu feugiat nulla facilisis at vero eros et accumsan et iusto odio dignissim qui blandit praesent luptatum zzril delenit augue duis dolore te feugait nulla facilisi.

Lorem ipsum dolor sit amet adipiscing

Nam liber tempor cum soluta nobis eleifend option congue nihil imperdiet doming id quod wisi enim ad minim veniam, quis nostrud exerci ut tation ullamcorper suscipit lobortis nisl ut aliquip ex ea commodo consequat.

Duis autem vel eum iriure dolor in hendrerit in vulputate velit esse molestie consequat, Ut wisi Lorem ipsum dolor sit amet, consectetuer adipiscing elit, sed

Duis autem vel eum iriure dolor in hendrerit in ut vulputate velit esse molestie consequat uat, vel illum dolore eu feugiat nulla facilisis.

Lorem ipsum dolor sit amet, consectetuer adipiscing elit, sed diam nonummy nibh euismod tincidunt ut laoreet dolore magna aliquam erat volutpat. Ut wisi enim ad minim veniam, quis nostrud exerci ut tation ullamcorper suscipit lobortis nisl ut aliquip ex ea commodo consequat.

Lorem ipsum dolor si

Duis autem vel eum iriure dolor in hendrerit in vulputate velit esse molestie consequat, Ut wisi Lorem ipsum dolor sit amet, consectetuer adipiscing elit, sed diam nonummy nibh euismod nostrud exerci ut tation ullamcorper suscipit lobortis nisl ut aliquip ex ea commodo consequat.

Ut wisi enim ad minim veniam, quis nostrud exerci ut tation ullamcorper suscipit lobortis nisl ut aliquip ex ea commodo consequat. Duis autem vel eum iriure dolor in hendrerit in vulputate velit esse molestie consequat, vel illum dolore eu feugiat nulla facilisis at vero eros et accumsan et iusto odio dignissim ut qui blandit praesent luptatum zzril delenit augue duis dolore te feugait nulla facilisi.

Lorem ipsum dolor consectetuer adipiscing

Lorem ipsum dolor sit amet, consectetuer adipiscing elit, sed diam nonummy nibh euismod tincidunt ut laoreet dolore magna aliquam erat volutpat. Ut wisi enim ad minim veniam, quis nostrud exerci ut tation ullamcorper suscipit lobortis nisl ut aliquip ex ea commodo consequat.

Lorem ipsum dolor sit amet, consectetuer adipiscing elit, sed diam nonummy nibh euismod tincidunt ut laoreet dolore magna aliquam erat volutpat. Ut wisi enim ad minim veniam, quis nostrud exerci ut tation ullamcorper suscipit lobortis nisl ut aliquip ex

Acme News is printed monthly for Ali Bakian and all the men and women of the Acme Widget Company. Lorem ipsum dolor sit amet, consectetuer adipiscing elit, sed diam nonummy nibh euismod tincidunt ut laoreet dolore magna aliquam erat volutpat. Ut wisi enim ad minim veniam, quis nostrud exerci ut tation ullamcorper suscipit lobortis nisl ut aliquip ex ea commodo consequat. Duis autem vel eum iriure dolor in hendrerit in vulputate velit esse molestie consequat, Ut wisi Lorem ipsum dolor sit amet, consectetuer adipiscing elit, sed diam nonummy nibh Duis autem vel eum iriure dolor in hendrerit in vulputate velit esse molestie consequat, Ut wisi Lorem ipsum dolor sit amet.

A Tip of the Hat

Duis autem vel eum iriure dolor in hen drerit in ut vulputate velit esse molestie cons equt uat, vel illum dolore nulla facilisis.

Lorem ipsum dolor sit amet, consectetuer adipiscing elit, sed diam nonummy nibh euismod tincidunt ut laoreet dolore magna aliquam erat volutpat. Ut wisi enim ad minim veniam, quis nostrud exerci ut tation ullamcorper ut ex ea commodo consequat.

Duis autem vel eum iriure dolor in hendrerit in vulputate velit esse molestie consequat, ut wisi lorem.

Acme News is printed monthly for Jenny Davis and all the men and women of the Acme Widget Company. Lorem ipsum dolor sit amet, consectetuer adipiscing elit, sed diam nonummy nibh euismod tincidunt ut laoreet dolore magna aliquam erat volutpat. Ut wisi enim ad minim veniam, quis nostrud exerci ut tation ullamcorper suscipit lobortis nisl ut aliquip ex ea commodo consequat. Duis autem vel eum iriure dolor in hendrerit in vulputate velit esse molestie consequat, Ut wisi Lorem ipsum dolor sit amet, consectetuer adipiscing elit, sed diam nonummy nibh Duis autem vel eum iriure dolor in hendrerit in vulputate velit esse molestie consequat, Ut wisi Lorem ipsum dolor sit

A Tip of the Hat

Duis autem vel eum iriure dolor in hen drerit in ut vulputate velit esse molestie cons equt uat, vel illum dolore nulla facilisis.

Lorem ipsum dolor sit amet, consectetuer adipiscing elit, sed diam nonummy nibh euismod tincidunt ut laoreet dolore magna aliquam erat volutpat. Ut wisi enim ad minim veniam, quis nostrud exerci ut tation ullamcorper ut ex ea commodo consequat.

Duis autem vel eum iriure dolor in hendrerit in vulputate velit esse molestie consequat, ut wisi lorem.

4. Division of space

Almost all newsletters use a columnar division of space, and almost all of them use a one-, two-, or three-column **grid**. Each of these is appropriate for a newsletter. It depends on the look you are trying to achieve. Consider how your readers perceive each grid and identify the one that will help you reach your objective.

A one-column grid suggests a newsy and informational tone. It is also the easiest grid to design because you have the fewest design decisions to make. If you are up against a deadline all the time, have little or no art, are typing your newsletter, or prefer a "newsy"

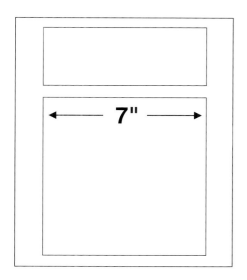

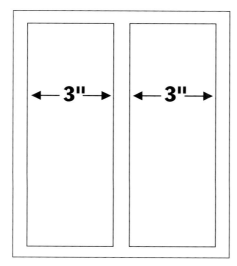

format, you should be using a one-column grid.

A two-column grid is perceived by your readers as formal, conservative, and technical. It is the most dignified and stately grid alternative and is an effective way to convey a sense of tradition.

A three-column grid creates the opposite image. It's perceived as relaxed, friendly, accessible, and casual. Use a three-column grid to convey a sense of neighborliness, imply ease of access, or suggest, "We're here to help."

Notice that the issue isn't whether *you're* formal or casual, technical or accessible; rather, the issue is what image do you want to convey?

A pharmaceutical company, for example, published a newsletter targeting diabetics. They easily could have selected a two-column grid to convey the idea of "The best science money can buy" – but they didn't. By using a three-column newsletter instead, they sent the message, "You can live a normal life with our help."

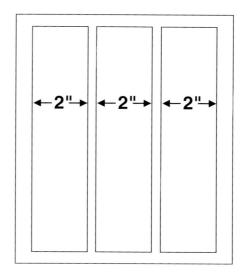

A scholar's margin is the best way to lighten up a dense layout. The term "scholar's margin" refers to any division of space that has one narrow column and one or two wider columns. You can either leave the narrow column blank or fill it in a little bit.

Note that the example on page 46, "Templine" uses a scholar's margin grid. This division of space works well when it's left completely empty. But it also works well when it's used to highlight certain sections of content.

For example, you could use the narrow column for the table of contents on the front page; or for author's photos and biographical information; or for pull quotes, tips, sidebars, or summary

Using a scholar's margin grid on the front page works well with any other grid used throughout the rest of the newsletter. Another option is to use the scholar's margin throughout the newsletter.

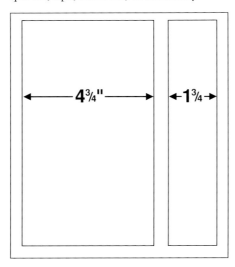

bullet points. You can see how versatile a tool this grid alternative is.

Use a scholar's margin grid when the amount of copy varies from issue to issue. The narrow column allows flexibility. By positioning a sidebar in the narrow margin, for instance, you can summarize key points when you're short sufficient text to fill the space, or delete the sidebar completely when you need the column for regular content.

As you review and compare these examples, notice how professional they appear. The scholar's margin grid

allows for varying amounts of content while maintaining harmony throughout. Whether the narrow column is left completely empty, used for regular content only periodically, used to highlight certain sections of content (such as pull quotes), or serves to illustrate what the content describes (such as showing computer monitor images, for example), the grid allotment of space opens up the layout, adding complexity and visual interest without requiring too much effort or time to design.

You can use more than one grid in your design, if you are careful and consistent. If it is not done with care and competence, your newsletter could look amateurish.

For instance, you can put the question and answer column in a three-column grid to make it seem user-friendly, or set the "President's Letter" in one column so that it will be perceived as "newsy."

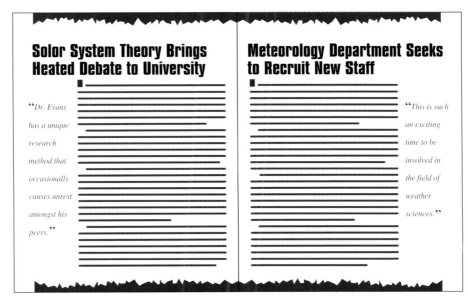

When designing with a scholar's margin, you can lay it out either narrow/wide, narrow/wide, or narrow/wide, wide/narrow. As with most aspects of design, it matters less what you do than that you do it consistently.

Leave the scholar's margin blank or mostly blank to open up the layout and make it look accessible.

With a scholar's margin grid, it's usually best to use a scholar's margin on the cover with a two- or three-column grid thereafter, or to use the scholar's margin grid throughout.

Simplicity is always a virtue in design, so don't combine grids simply to show off your computer's technology or "for variety."

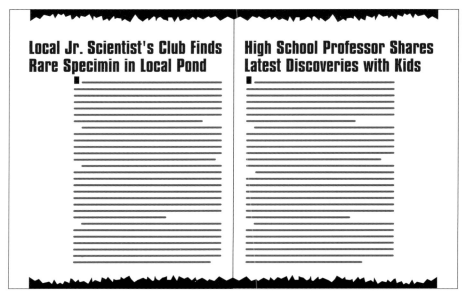

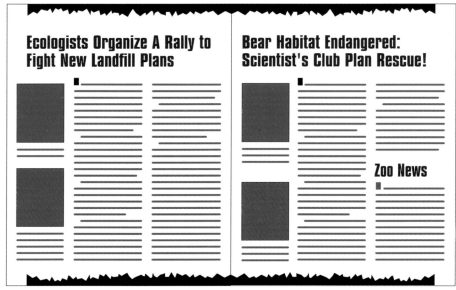

5. Type

Type is the most important design element, because it directly affects the newsletter's readability.

Adhering to the rules of readability is important, but you do not have to follow them all rigidly. Remember, however, that every time you break a rule, you are making your newsletter a little less readable. The topic of readability has been thoroughly researched. Follow the rules and your newsletter will be readable.

There are two broad categories of type: **serif** and **sans serif**. Letters in a serif font seems to be standing on platforms, and some parts of the letters are thinner than other parts. In a sans serif font, letters have no thick or thin parts and there are no platforms. (*Sans* in French means "without.")

Serif
Sans Serif

People read sans serif type faster than they read serif, but with less accuracy because the hooks and feet of a serif font serve as a kind of "picket fence" that guides the eye.

President's Letter

President's Letter

acher's Report

Whenever you begin to specify the type you will use ("speccing type"), start with body text. A serif font should be used in body text, because its picket fence effect makes it easy to read.

Next choose your headline font, which usually will be a sans serif. Because readers are more likely to read headlines than anything else, they should be able to do so easily and quickly. When they have made the commitment to read the body of the text, they need the enhanced readability that comes from a serif font. These two selections, a sans serif for the headlines and a serif for the body text, are the two primary fonts that are needed in a newsletter. (Whatever you select for your nameplate or your standing heads doesn't count, as the nameplate and standing heads are graphic elements.)

You should select standing head fonts to create a strong image. Standing heads are perceived as independent elements, so their fonts can vary. A bold outline font might be appropriate for the "President's Letter," to convey the company's image of strength and boldness. An elegant script could be used to convey a feminine spirit for a cosmetics firm. Tekton type (the third example above) could be used for the "Teacher's Report" along with a plump, polished apple.

Notice how different from one another these three standing heads are. Type does an excellent job of conveying an image or getting attention.

55

Each font is set in 20 point type. Look at the profoundly different amount of space taken by each lower case alphabet.

Avant Garde
abcdefghijklmnopqrstuvwxyz

Century Old Style
abcdefghijklmnopqrstuvwxyz

COPPERPLATE 33BC
ABCDEFGHIJKLMNOPQRSTUVWXYZ

Garamond
abcdefghijklmnopqrstuvwxyz

Helvetica
abcdefghijklmnopqrstuvwxyz

Palatino
abcdefghijklmnopqrstuvwxyz

Tekton
abcdefghijklmnopqrstuvwxyz

Type is measured by **point** size, as it has been since type was set by hand. One point is equal to ½ of an inch. Body text should be set between 9 and 12 points, but keep in mind that fonts are individually designed elements, the same copy set in the same size in different fonts will take up different amounts of space.

A good choice for general audiences is 12-point type. People who read well and see well can read 10-point type. But such readers would probably be between 18 and 35 years of age, as you generally should assume people under 18 years of age do not read well and people over 35 years of age do not see well.

The New York Times large print edition, which targets older readers and the visually disabled, is set in 18 points. However, most organizations which assist the visually disabled use type no larger than 16 points. If your readers are over 55, it is reasonable to set the print at 14 to 18 points, but in no case should you go larger.

At the smaller end of the spectrum, do not set newsletter body text smaller than 9 points, no matter how well your readers read and see. The only exceptions to this rule would be when you have so much extra copy that even after adjusting the leading, alleys, margins, and gutters, there is not enough space to print it, or when you want to convey a sense of depth of content or technical sophistication.

A church newsletter broke the nine-point rule for another reason. The newsletter was sent to the entire congregation, but the singles group wanted to sponsor a series of events targeting only those under 35 years old. Concerned about issues of age discrimination, the group ran the articles announcing the singles events in the newsletter set in 8-point type — which could be easily deciphered only by the age group they were targeting.

Once you have decided on body text size, you can calculate the size of headings. Subheads need to be two to four points larger than the body text. Headlines need to be at least twice the size of subheads. For example, if you are using 12-point type in your body text, the subheads should be at least 14 points, and the headlines should be at least 28 points.

You can experiment with more than these three basic levels of distinction: body text, subheads, and headlines. For example, you could have the body

text set in 12 points, with the first two lines (the journalistic "lead in") enlarged to 14 points. The subheads might be 18 points and the headline 36. A biographical note about the author at the end of the article could be set in 10 points. In this instance, there would be five levels of type size, which is fine as long as consistency is maintained throughout the newsletter and in every issue of the newsletter. In fact, this is an excellent way to add professional pizazz to the newsletter.

Using a variety of **versions**, weights, and sizes of your two primary fonts adds complexity, but not confusion, to the newsletter.

Don't be inconsistent in the size of body text within an article or within your newsletter. Point size is sometimes reduced for copyfitting purposes, but there are better ways to handle this problem.

10/12 type:

Lorem ipsum dolor et sit amet, con sectetur adipscing elit, sed diam nonnumy eiusmod tempor incidunt ut labore et dolore magna aliquam erat volupat. Ut enim ad minimim veni ami quis nostnud exercitation ullam corpor sus cipit laboris nisi ut aliquip ex ea commodo et consequat. Duisa utem vel eum irure dolor in repre henderit in voluptate velit esse mol estaie son consequat, vel illum dolore eu fugiat nulla pariatur. At vero eos et accusam et justo odio dig nissim qui blandit praesent lupatum delenit duos dolor et molestais exceptur occaecat cupidat non provident, simil tempor sunt in culpa qui officia desenunt moll anim id est labonum dolor fugai.

10/11.5 type:

Lorem ipsum dolor et sit amet, con sectetur adipscing elit, sed diam nonnumy eiusmod tempor incidunt ut labore et dolore magna aliquam erat volupat. Ut enim ad minimim veni ami quis nostnud exercitation ullam corpor sus cipit laboris nisi ut aliquip ex ea commodo et consequat. Duisa utem vel eum irure dolor in repre henderit in voluptate velit esse mol estaie son consequat, vel illum dolore eu fugiat nulla pariatur. At vero eos et accusam et justo odio dig nissim qui blandit praesent lupatum delenit duos dolor et molestais exceptur occaecat cupidat non provident, simil tempor sunt in culpa qui officia desenunt moll anim id est labonum dolor fugai.

Your newsletter isn't a brochure or ad, even if it has selling objectives. Be sure it's readable and not too jazzy-looking.

One of the ways to make copy fit better without reducing the point size is to reduce the **leading** or line spacing. In newsletter body text, you'll want to use between one and three points of leading. To decide what leading to use, consider three things: the font, its size, and copyfitting.

The font you are using is the first consideration. For example, if you decide to use a sans serif font for the body text rather than the recommended serif font, then you should add extra leading, two or three points, to compensate for the reduced readability.

The next consideration is the size of the font. The general rule is that the larger the font, the more white space between lines it can support. If you use 9-point type and 3 points of leading, then the space between the lines is a third the size of the font. On the other hand, if you use 12-point type, 3 points of leading is only a quarter of the type size.

The final consideration is copyfitting. If you have too much copy to fit comfortably in the available space, reduce leading by half a point. A half a point of space allotted for every line will greatly increase the amount of space available for text. Remember, you should reduce type size for copyfitting

purposes only as a last resort.

In the language of leading, one says "10 on 12" (10-point type with two points of leading) or "11 on 12" (11-point type with one point of leading). The second number is the sum of the type size and the leading. When speccing the type, we write it with numbers and a slash. "10/12" means 10-point type with two points of leading.

Another type-related decision involves column justification. Avoid setting a "ragged" left margin (where the left margin of type is uneven, not aligned) — it is extremely hard to read. If you are using a word processor to produce your newsletter, you *must* use a ragged right margin, like in the example above, because word processing programs are not good at justification. They produce rivers of **white space**

Lorem ipsum dolor sit amet, consectetur adipscing elit, sed diam nonnumy eiusmod tempor incidunt ut labore et dolore magna aliquam erat volupat. Ut enim ad minimim veniami quis nostnud exercitation ullamcorpor suscipit laboris nisi ut aliquip ex ea commodo consequat. Duis autem vel eum irure dolor in reprehenderit in voluptate velit esse molestaie son consequat, vel illum dolore eu fugiat nulla pariatur. At vero eos et accusam et justo odio dignissim qui

which distract the reader's eye and diminish readership.

However, if you are using a good desktop publishing program, or if you are having the newsletter professionally typeset, you can use either ragged or justified right margins.

Decisions about right margin justification should be based on the image you want to create. Just as a two-column grid is perceived as formal, conservative, and technical, so too is a layout set with a justified right margin. A ragged right margin, like a three-column grid, is seen as relaxed, friendly, and casual. When you match these two elements in your newsletter, you are sending two graphic signals that combine to convey a powerful message.

Mixing and matching these two elements is rarely a good idea. It adds a complexity to the design that is rarely appropriate in a newsletter. It is better to save that level of depth and sophistication for brochures, catalogs, and ads.

However, one reason to consider breaking this rule is if you need to reach different audience segments with one newsletter. For instance, a technical update column targeting non-technical readers might be put in a three-column ragged right margin layout and will convey a sense of relaxed ease-of-use. Next to it, there could be a sidebar set in a right-justified column containing information specific for technical users. This layout combines newsiness (one-column grid) with technical expertise (justified right column). Be sure to use caution when combining different grids, so that

Wow! Newsletters Get Read

Futura font

Wow! Newsletters Get Read

Palatino font

Lorem ipsum dolor sit amet, consectetur adipscing elit, sed diam nonnumy eiusmod tempor incidunt ut labore et dolore magna aliquam erat volupat. Ut enim ad minimim veniami quis nostnud exercitation ullamcorpor suscipit laboris nisi ut aliquip ex ea commodo consequat. Duis autem vel eum irure dolor in reprehenderit in voluptate velit esse molestaie son consequat, vel illum dolore eu fugiat nulla pariatur. At vero eos et accusam et justo odio dignissim qui

For optimum readability, you need to use a highly legible font. Notice that the "a" in Futura is rounded, while the "a" in Palatino has a high second story. Also the "e" in Futura has a tight opening compared to the "e" in Palatino. The "o" is rounded in Futura, whereas there is an elliptical center which tilts to the left in Palatino. When these three lowercase letters, the most common in English, are rounded and alike, the font is not legible enough for use in a newsletter.

you don't confuse your readers or look as though you are just showcasing your computer's technical abilities.

Indent paragraphs in your newsletter for maximum readability. An indentation of four to five characters increases readability by seven percent. If space allows it, add a little extra space between paragraphs as well. In publishing convention, you never indent a first paragraph, but you do indent all others. It's your decision whether or not to follow this convention, but if you do, it should be done consistently in every article throughout your newsletter.

Italics are hard to read. You should assume that ten words or more set in italics won't be read.

Make sure that captions are readable and that they look different from the body text, because they are more likely to be read than the body text. Here are two good options for captions: Set your body text font in bold and change the size, or reduce your headline font to the size of the body text and set it in bold. **Italics** are not a good choice for captions. Choose italics only to emphasize a word or two, for a title, or to highlight a certain category of content.

Four to five characters

Lorem ipsum dolor sit amet, consectetur adipscing elit, sed diam nonnumy eiusmod tempor incidunt ut labore et dolore magna aliquam erat volupat. Ut enim ad minimim veniami quis nostnud exercitation ullamcorpor suscipit laboris nisi ut aliquip ex ea commodo consequat.

Duis autem vel eum irure dolor in reprehenderit in voluptate velit esse molestaie son consequat, vel illum dolore eu fugiat nulla pariatur. At vero eos et accusam et just diodignissim.

For instance, consider this approach in a newsletter: Set each author's byline in italics, all references to someone's name and job title in small caps (capital letters that are only as tall as lower case letters), and product names in bold. These three tools used for emphasis throughout the newsletter, and used consistently in every issue of the newsletter, add panache while still using only one font.

Setting headlines in all caps (capital letters) conveys a powerful image, but it is hard to read. Be cautious, also, about using decorative, ornate, or specialty fonts in either body text or headlines. However, they can be used effectively in standing heads or to highlight a few key words. For example, for an upcoming Renaissance Fair you could set the R and F of those two words in a Gothic face such as London for an interesting and dramatic effect.

As you consider which fonts to select for your newsletter, keep the rules we have reviewed in mind. It's not necessary to be limited by these choices. You now know enough about readability and **legibility** to choose from among the thousands of alternatives available. For example, if you want to consider Helvetica, type out the letters from A to Z and consider how they look. Do they look modern? How about Goudy? Is it elegant? Traditional? Now consider legibility. Consider each font's lowercase a, e, and o.

Armed with the information covered in this section, you are in a position to make thoughtful, considered decisions that will help your newsletter achieve its objectives.

In just a moment, turn to the next two pages for a second or two. Do not look for any detail, only for an overall impression of the two samples. After a brief look, decide which one you would rather read. When you have made your decision, look at the samples in more detail and read the related text. Please flash open the page now, close the book while you decide, then continue reading.

Helvetica
ABCDEFGHIJKLMNOPQRSTUVWXYZ
The lazy brown fox jumped quickly over the sagging fence.

Goudy
ABCDEFGHIJKLMNOPQRSTUVWXYZ
The lazy brown fox jumped quickly over the sagging fence.

Contrast these two fonts: Notice how one is clean and modern-looking (Helvetica), and the other seems rich and luxurious (Goudy).

ANYTOWN
landscaping

MARCH 1996	VOLUME 2	NUMBER 1

Lorem ipsum dolor sit

Consectetuer adipiscing elit, seddiam nonummy nibh euismod tincidunt utlaoreet dolore magna aliquam eratvolutpat. Ut wisienimad minim veniam, quis nostrud exerciation ullamcorper suscipit lobortisnisl aliquip exea commodo consequat.

Duis autem vel eum iriure dolor hendrerit invulputate velit esse molestie con sequatvel illumre doloreeu feugiat nua facilisis vero eroset accumsanet iusto odio dignissim qui bladit prae sentluptum zzril delenit duis dolorete feugaitnulla facilisi. Lorem ipsumdolor sit amet, secteteur adipiscing elit, sed diam noumy esmod tincidunt laoreet doloremagna aliquam evolutpat.

Ut enim ad minim veniam, quinostrud exerci ut tation ullamcorper suscipit lobortis ut aliquip ea commodo consequat. Duis autem eumiriure dolor hendrerit in vulputate velit esse molestie consequat.

Duis autemvel iriure dolor inhendrerit inut vulputate velitesse molestie uat, veliillum dolore eufeugiat nulla facilisis.

Lorem ipsum dolor sit amet, con sectetuer adipiscing diam nomy nibheuis tinci duntut laoreet dolore magnaaliquam eratvolutpat. Ut wisienim minim veniam, quisnostrud exerci tation ullamcorper suscipitlobortis ut aliquipexea commodo consequat.

Duis autem veleuiure dor inhendret molestie consequat.

Lorem ipsum dolor sit consectetuer

Ut wisirem ipsum dolor sit amet, consectetuer aiscing elit, seddiam nonuy heuod nostud exerciut tation ullcorper suscipit lobortis nisl aliquipex eacodo consequat. Ut enimad minim veniam, quis nostrud exercit tation ullamcoer suscipit lobortis nislut aliquip exea commo consequat. Duis autem veleum iriure dolor hendrerit inputate velit esse molestie consequ velillum doloreeu feugialla facili atvero eroset accumsan etisto utqui blandit praesent lupta zzrillenit auguduis dolore te feugait nulla facili.

Nam libertempor cum soluta nobis eleifend optcongue nihil imperdiet domingid quod enimad veniamquis nostrud exerci utation ullamcorper cipit nisl utaliqui pex eamodo consequat.

Lorem ipsum dolsit amet, conseer adipiscing elitsed diam nonummy nibh eod tincidunt laoreetdolore id magna aliquam volutpatrue.

Duis autem iriure dolor inhendrerit in vulputate velit esse molestie consequat, vel dolore feugiat nulla facilisis vero eros et accmsan et iusto dignissim qui blanditprae sent.

Lorem dolor sit consectetuer

Duis autem vel iriure dolor inhendrerit vulputate velit esse molestie consequat, dolore feugiat nulla facilisis vero eros accumsan iusto dignissim qui blaprae sent luptatum delenit augueduis dolore feugait nulla facilisi. Lorem ipsum dolor amet, consectetuer adipcing ed diam nonumy nib euismd tincidunt utlaoreet dolore mag aliquam volutpat. Ut enim minim veniam, quis nostrd exerci tation ullamcorper suscipit lobortis aliquip ex comodo consequat. Duis autem vel eum iriure hendrerit in vulputate velit esse molestie consequat, illum dolore feugiatnulla facilisis vero eros accumsan et iusto dignissim qui blandit praesent lum zzril delenit augue duis dolore nul.

Ipsum Consectetuer

Nam liber tempor soluta nobis eld option congue nihil impdiet dom id quod wisi enim ad veniam, quis nostru erci ut tation ullarper suscipit lobortis nisl ut aliquip ex commodo consequat.

Duis autem eum iriure dolor in hendrerit vulputate vel esse molestie con sequt uat, illum dolore eu feugiat nulla facilisis.

Which one did you feel inclined to read? Most likely, you chose the yellow one. Most people want to read black type on white paper, and of these two examples, the yellow one is closer to the desirable black on white.

However, if you look at these examples in more detail, you might become attracted to the green. There are at least four reasons for this phenomenon. See if you can identify all four before reading on.

First of all, the yellow newsletter is set in sans serif, the green in serif. The yellow's font is 8 points and the green's is 10 points. The yellow's has too much leading, eight on eleven, whereas the green's is set ten on eleven. Both the yellow and green newsletters are justified, but the hyphenation was turned off in the yellow one, creating irritating and distracting rivers of white space.

Also notice the difference in the alleys. This would be a major problem in the yellow newsletter if not for the strong **rule** separating the columns of text. Also, the paragraphing is odd.

Keep in mind how easy it would be, with a pull-down menu or the push of a button, to create something as unreadable as this yellow newsletter. It's not that the green newsletter is ideal, but it's better than the yellow one!

Never let technology dictate design — *you* dictate design. The fact that your computer can do something isn't a good enough reason to do it.

ANYTOWN
landscaping

| MARCH 1996 | VOLUME 2 | NUMBER 1 |

Lorem ipsum dolor consectetuer

Lorem ipsum dolor sit amet, consectetuer adipiscing elit, sed diam nonummy nibh euismod tincidunt ut laoreet dolore magna aliquam erat volutpat. Ut wisi enim ad minim veniam, quis nostrud exerci tation ullamcorper suscipit lobortis nisl ut aliquip ex commodo consequat.

Duis autem vel eum iriure dolor in hendrerit in vulputate velit esse molestie consequat, vel illum dolore eu feugiat nulla facilisis at vero eros et accumsan et iusto odio dignissim qui blandit praesent luptatum zzril delenit augue duis dolore te feugait nulla fac ilisi. Lorem ip sum elit, sed diam nibh euismod tincidunt erat volutpat.

Ut wisi enim ad minim veniam, quis nostrud exerci ut tation aliquip ex ea commod.

Lorem ipsum

Duis autem vel eum iriure dolor in hendrerit in vulputate velit esse molestie consequat, vel illum dolore eu feugiat nulla facilisis at vero eros.

Nam liber tempor cum soluta nobis eleifend option congue nihil imperdiet doming id quod wisi enim ad minim veniam.

Lorem ipsum dolor consectetuer

Duis autem vel eum iriure dolor in hendrerit in ut vulputate velit esse molestie consequt uat, vel illum dolore eu feugiat nulla facilisis.

Lorem ipsum dolor sit amet, consectetuer adipiscing elit, sed diam nonummy nibh euismod tincidunt ut laoreet dolore magna aliquam erat volutpat. Ut wisi enim ad minim veniam, quis nostrud exerci ut tation ullamcorper suscipit lobortis nisl ut aliquip ex ea commodo consequat. Duis autem vel eum iriure dolor in hendrerit in vulputate velit esse molestie consequat, Ut wisi dolor sit amet, consectetuer adipiscing elit, sed dim nonummy.

Ut wisi enim ad minim veniam, quis nostrud exerci ut tation ullamcorper suscipit lobortis nisl ut aliquip ex ea commodo consequat.

Lorem ipsum dolor et amet consectetuer

Et vero eros et accumsan et iusto odio dignissim ut qui blandit praesent luptatum zzril delenit augue duis dolore te feugait nulla facilisi.

Nam liber tempor cum soluta nobis eleifend option congue nihil imperdiet doming id quod wisi enim ad minim veniam, quis nostrud exerci ut tation ullamcorper suscipit lobortis.

Lorem ipsum dolor sit amet, consectetuer adipiscing elit, sed diam nonummy nibh euismod tincidunt ut.

Ut wisi enim ad minim veniam, quis nostrud exerci tation ullamcorper suscipit lobortis nisl ut aliquip ex ea commodo consequat.

Lorem ipsum

iure dolor in hendrerit in vulputate velit esse molestie consequat, vel illum dolore eu feugiat nu lla facilisis at vero eros et accumsan et iusto odio dignissim qui

Consider this copy-heavy newsletter. It's set in Times-Roman, ten on eleven. There is a nice alley, a strong rule, and a little **inish cap.** The objective of the newsletter is to sell the books dis-cussed. Compare the page on the left with a later page of the same newsletter, at right. Do you see what happened? The newsletter editor had too much copy, so he reduced the point size. To make matters worse, it decreases gradually from ten to nine to eight to seven. Readers know nothing about type, but they know whether they want to read it or not!

---

exerci tation ullamcorper suscipit lobortis nisl ut aliquip ex ea commodo consequat. Duis autem vel eum iriure dolor in hendrerit in vulputate velit esse molestie consequat, vel illum dolore eu feugiat nulla facilisis at vero eros et accumsan et iusto odio dignissim qui blandit praesent luptatum zzril duis dolore te feugait nulla facilisi.

Lorem ipsum dolor sit amet, consectetuer adipiscing elit, sed diam nonummy nibh euismod tincidunt ut laoreet dolore magna aliquam erat volutpat. Ut wisi enim ad minim veniam, quis nostrud exerci tation ullamcorper suscipit lobortis nisl ut aliquip ex ea commodo consequat. Duis autem vel eum iriure dolor in hendrerit in vulputate velit esse molestie consequat, vel illum dolore eu feugiat nulla facilisis at vero eros et accumsan et iusto odio dignissim qui

blandit praesent luptatum zzril delenit augue duis dolore te feugait nulla facilisi. Nam liber tempor cum soluta nobis eleifend option congue nihil imperdiet doming id quod mazim placerat facer possim assum. Lorem ipsum dolor sit amet, consectetuer adipiscing elit, sed diam nonummy nibh euismod tincidunt ut laoreet dolore magna aliquam erat volutpat. Ut wisi enim ad minim veniam, quis nostrud exerci tation ullamcorper suscipit lobortis nisl ut aliquip ex ea commodo consequat. Duis autem vel eum iriure dolor in hendrerit in vulputate velit orem ipsum dolor sit amet, con sectetuer adipiscing elit, sed diam nonummy nibh euismod tincidunt ut laoreet dolore magna aliquam erat volutpat. Ut wisi enim ad minim veniam, quis nostrud exerci tation ullamcorper suscipit lobortis nisl ut aliquip ex ea commodo consequat. Duis autem vel eum iriure dolor in hendrerit in vulputate velit esse molestie consequat, vel illum dolore eu feugiat nulla facilisis.Lorem ipsum dolor sit amet, consectetuer adipiscing elit, sed diam nonummy mmodo consequat.

Attilio Bertolucci

La camera da letto

Parma and the Past, the Poet.

• 256 pp. Milan: Garzanti, L20,000

Attilio Bertolucci, lorem ipsum dolor sit amet, con sect etuer adipiscing elit, sed diam nonummy nibh euismod tincidunt ut laoreet dolore magna aliquam erat volutpat. Ut wisi enim ad minim veniam, quis nostrud exerci tation ullamcorper suscipit lobortis nisl ut aliquip ex ea commodo consequat. Duis autem vel eum iriure dolor in vulputate velit esse molestie consequat, vel illum dolore eu feugiat nulla facilisis at vero eros et accumsan et iusto odio dignissim qui blandit praesent luptatum zzril delenit augue duis dolore te feugait nulla facilisi. Lorem ipsum dolor sit amet, consectetuer adipiscing elit, sed diam nonummy nibh euismod tincidunt ut laoreet dolore magna aliquam erat volutpat. Ut wisi enim ad minim veniam, quis nostrud exerci tation ullamcorper suscipit lobortis nisl ut aliquip ex ea commodo consequat. Duis autem vel eum iriure dolor in hendrerit in vulputate velit esse molestie consequat, vel illum dolore eu feugiat nulla facilisis at vero eros et accumsan et iusto odio dignissim qui blandit praesent luptatum zzril delenit augue duis dolore te feugait nulla facilisi.

Nam liber tempor cum soluta nobis eleifend option congue nihil imperdiet doming id quod mazim placerat facer possim assum. Lorem ipsum dolor sit amet, consectetuer adipiscing elit, sed diam nonummy nibh euismod tincidunt ut laoreet dolore magna aliquam erat volutpat. Ut wisi enim ad minim veniam, quis nostrud exerci tation ullamcorper suscipit lobortis nisl ut aliquip ex ea commodo consequat. Duis autem vel eum iriure dolor in hendrerit in vulputate velit esse molestie consequat, vel illum dolore eu feugiat

nulla facilisis at vero eros et accumsan et iusto odio dignissim qui blandit praesent luptatum zzril delenit augue duis dolore te feugait nulla facilisi. Lorem ipsum dolor sit amet, consectetuer adipiscing elit, sed diam nonummy nibh eui ut dolore magna aliquam erat volutpat.

Ut wisi enim ad minim veniam, quis nostrud exerci tation ullamcorper suscipit lobortis nisl ut aliquip ex ea commodo consequat. Duis autem vel eum iriure dolor in hendrerit in vulputate velit esse molestie consequat, vel illum dolore eu feugiat nulla facilisis at vero eros et accumsan et iusto odio dignissim qui blandit praesent luptatum zzril delenit augue duis dolore te feugait nulla facilisi.

Nam liber tempor cum soluta nobis eleifend option congue nihil imperdiet doming id quod ma zim placerat facer possim assum. Lorem ipsum dolor sit amet, consectetuer adipiscing elit, sed diam nonummy nibh euismod tincidunt ut laoreet dolore magna aliquam erat volutpat.

Ut wisi enim ad minim veniam, quis nostrud exerci tation ullamcorper suscipit lobortis nisl ut aliquip ex ea commodo consequat. Duis autem vel eum iriure dolor in vulputate velit esse molestie consequat, vel illum dolore eu feugiat nulla facilisis. Lorem ipsum dolor sit amet, consectetuer adipiscing elit, sed diam nonummy nibh euismod tincidunt ut laoreet dolore magna aliquam erat volutpat. Ut wisi enim ad minim veniam, quis nostrud exerci tation ullamcorper suscipit lobortis nisl ut aliquip ex ea commodo consequat. Lorem ipsum dolor sit amet, consectetuer adipiscing elit, sed diam nonummy nibh euismod tincidunt ut laoreet dolore magna aliquam erat volutpat. Ut wisi enim ad minim veniam, quis nostrud

---

Romeo De Maio

La donna nil Rinascimento

Sei l'amica del demonio

Lorem ipsum dolor sit amet, con sectetuer adipiscing elit, sed diam nonummy nibh euismod tincidunt ut laoreet dolore magna aliquam erat volutpat. Ut wisi enim ad minim veniam, quis nostrud exerci tation ullamcorper suscipit lobortis nisl ut aliquip ex ea commodo consequat. Duis autem vel eum iriure dolor in hendrerit in vulputate velit esse molestie consequat, vel illum dolore eu feugiat nulla facilisis at vero eros et accumsan et iusto odio dignissim qui blandit praesent orem ipsum dolor sit amet, con sectetuer adipiscing elit, sed diam nonummy nibh euismod tincidunt ut laoreet dolore magna aliquam erat volutpat. Ut wisi enim ad minim veniam, quis nostrud exerci tation ullamcorper suscipit lobortis nisl ut aliquip ex ea commodo consequat.

Duis autem vel eum iriure dolor in hendrerit in vulputate velit esse molestie consequat, vel illum dolore eu feugiat nulla facilisis at vero eros et accumsan et iusto odio dignissim qui blandit praesent luptatum zzril delenit augue duis dolore te feugait nulla facilisi. Lorem ipsum dolor sit amet, consectetuer adipiscing elit, sed diam nonummy nibh euismod tincidunt ut laoreet dolore magna aliquam erat volutpat. Ut wisi enim ad minim veniam, quis nostrud exerci tation ullamcorper suscipit lobortis nisl ut aliquip ex ea commodo consequat. Duis autem vel eum iriure dolor in hendrerit in vulputate velit esse molestie consequat, vel illum dolore eu feugiat nulla facilisis at vero eros et accumsan et iusto odio dignissim qui blandit praesent luptatum zzril delenit augue duis dolore te feugait nulla facilisi.

Nam liber tempor cum soluta nobis eleifend option congue nihil imperdiet doming id quod mazim placerat facer possim assum.

Lorem ipsum dolor sit amet, consectetuer adipiscing elit, sed diam nonummy nibh euismod tincidunt ut laoreet dolore magna aliquam erat volutpat. Ut wisi enim ad minim veniam, quis nostrud exerci tation ullamcorper suscipit lobortis nisl ut aliquip ex ea commodo consequat.

Duis autem vel eum iriure dolor in hendrerit in vulputate velit esse molestie consequat, vel illum dolore eu feugiat nulla facilisis. Lorem ipsum dolor sit amet, consectetuer adipiscing elit, sed diam nonummy nibh euismod tincidunt ut laoreet dolore magna aliquam erat volutpat. Ut wisi enim ad minim veniam, quis nostrud exerci tation ullamcorper suscipit lobortis nisl ut aliquip ex ea commodo consequat. Duis autem vel eum iriure dolor in hendrerit in vulputate velit esse molestie consequat, vel illum dolore eu feugiat nulla facilisis.

elit, sed diam nonummy nibh euismod tincidunt ut laoreet dolore magna aliquam erat volutpat.

Ut wisi enim ad minim veniam, quis nostrud exerci tation ullamcorper suscipit lobortis nisl ut aliquip ex ea commodo consequat. Duis autem vel eum iriure dolor in hendrerit in vulputate velit esse molestie consequat, vel illum dolore eu feugiat nulla facilisis.

Lorem ipsum dolor sit amet, consectetuer adipiscing elit, sed diam nonummy nibh euismod tincidunt ut laoreet dolore magna aliquam erat volutpat. Ut wisi enim ad minim veniam, quis nostrud exerci tation ullamcorper suscipit lobortis nisl ut aliquip ex ea commodo consequat. Lorem ipsum dolor sit amet, consectetuer adipiscing elit, sed diam nonummy nibh euismod tincidunt ut laoreet dolore magna aliquam erat volutpat.

Ut wisi enim ad minim veniam, quis nostrud exerci tation ullamcorper suscipit lobortis nisl ut aliquip ex ea commodo consequat. Duis autem vel eum iriure dolor in hendrerit in vulputate velit esse molestie consequat, vel illum dolore eu feugiat nulla facilisis at vero eros et accumsan et iusto odio dignissim qui blandit praesent luptatum zzril delenit augue duis dolore te feugait nulla facilisi. Lorem ipsum dolor sit amet, consectetuer adipiscing elit, sed diam nonummy nibh euismod tincidunt ut laoreet dolore magna aliquam erat volutpat. Ut wisi enim ad minim veniam, quis nostrud exerci tation ullamcorper suscipit lobortis nisl ut aliquip ex ea commodo consequat. Duis autem vel eum iriure dolor in hendrerit in vulputate velit esse molestie consequat, vel illum dolore eu feugiat nulla facilisis.Lorem ipsum dolor sit amet, consectetuer adipiscing elit, sed diam nonummy mmodo consequat.

Duis autem vel eum iriure dolor in hendrerit in vulputate velit esse molestie consequat, vel illum dolore eu feugiat nulla facilisis at vero eros et accumsan et iusto odio dignissim qui blandit praesent luptatum zzril delenit augue duis dolore te feugait nulla facilisi. Lorem ipsum dolor sit amet, consectetuer adipiscing elit, sed diam nonummy nibh euismod tincidunt ut laoreet dolore magna aliquam erat volutpat. Ut wisi enim ad minim veniam, quis nostrud exerci tation ullamcorper suscipit lobortis nisl ut aliquip ex ea commodo consequat. Duis autem vel eum iriure dolor in hendrerit in vulputate velit esse molestie consequat, vel illum dolore eu feugiat nulla facilisis at vero eros et accumsan et iusto odio dignissim qui blandit praesent luptatum zzril delenit augue duis dolore te feugait nulla facilisi.

Nam liber tempor cum soluta nobis eleifend option congue nihil imperdiet doming id quod mazim placerat facer possim assum. Lorem ipsum dolor sit amet, consectetuer adipiscing elit, sed diam nonummy nibh euismod tincidunt ut laoreet dolore magna aliquam erat volutpat. Ut wisi enim ad minim veniam, quis nostrud exerci tation ullamcorper suscipit lobortis nisl ut aliquip ex ea commodo consequat. Duis autem vel eum iriure dolor in hendrerit in vulputate velit esse molestie consequat, vel illum dolore eu feugiat nulla facilisis at vero eros et accumsan et iusto odio dignissim qui blandit praesent luptatum zzril delenit augue duis dolore te feugait nulla facilisi. Lorem ipsum dolor sit amet, consectetuer adipiscing elit, sed diam nonummy nibh eui ut dolore magna aliquam erat volutpat.

Ut wisi enim ad minim veniam, quis nostrud exerci tation ullamcorper suscipit lobortis nisl ut aliquip ex ea commodo consequat. Duis autem vel

Remember to be careful about breaking too many rules of readability. Every time you break one, on some marginal level, you're creating something that's hard to read. While type can help call attention to your newsletter or create a strong image, you have to balance your desire to create something that's graphically interesting with the value of keeping your publication highly readable.

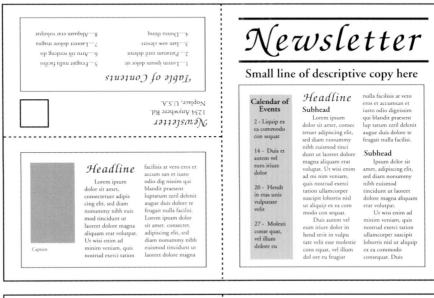

Headlines:
Zapf Chancery,
32 pt. on 36 pt. leading

Subheads:
Garamond Semibold,
16 pt. on 20 pt. leading

Body Copy:
Garamond Book,
12 pt. on 14 pt. leading

Captions:
Garamond Bold,
10 pt. on 11 pt. leading

Border:
1 pt. black frame

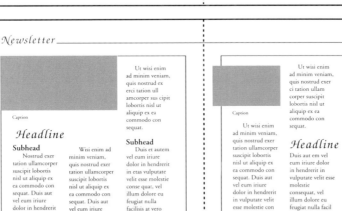

A visual spec sheet shows all of the decisions you have made, before the newsletter is printed. Before printing, ask the Editorial Advisory Board to look at the spec sheet. Also, check to see that the fonts you've selected are installed in your computer or otherwise available.

6. Graphic devices

Graphic devices are symbols that signal things to your reader. They serve multiple purposes: to help organize the layout, keep the content accessible, and help readers keep their place.

In a newsletter, it is best to limit yourself to two or three graphic devices and then apply them consistently throughout the newsletter, and in every issue of the newsletter. Keep the design simple. Too many graphic devices look fussy and may distract the reader. Remember that simplicity is a virtue in design.

Consider the Washington State Department of Social & Health Services newsletter. Look how much is accomplished with so few graphic devices. Notice how the two-column grid lends a certain formality. Observe also the multiple weights of rule (which count as one graphic device). The table of contents in this newsletter is titled "Inside."

On the inside page of the same issue, all caps is used for the standing head. As it's just one word, there is no readability issue, and it adds a touch of elegance consistent with the overall formal look of the newsletter. Notice how the photos are crossing the grid line. This serves to invite the reader in. The same weights of rules are used in the same locations as on the front page, surrounding the layout to contain the content and in the alley to separate the columns of text. Look at the **drop cap** and the black box used as a simple, yet elegant, stop device.

[Newsletter sample reproduction]

THE NETWORK NEWS

Washington State Department of Social and Health Services
Mental Health Division, Carrol Hernandez, Director

AUTUMN 1994

Work Group Examines Need For Comprehensive Crisis Re...

COMMENTARY

Emergency Services: One Less Barrier To Treatment

Pam Sloan
Director, Spokane Community Mental Health Center
Emergency Services

Jud Morris
Program Manager
Spokane County
Mental Health

Below is the calendar in a hotel's newsletter. See how the rules separate the columns of copy. This is a kind of scholar's margin — note the narrow left and right columns. The boxes with the dates in them look like an old-fashioned wall calendar with tear-off pages. The small white circles suggest rivets. Again, art that crosses the grid lines helps to invite the reader in.

A stop device is an effective way to signal to your readers where an article ends, before they've read a word. Position a small icon, your logo, a bullet, or a box at the end of each article, either at the end of the final line or immediately following the ending punctuation.

Notice that while the border is unique to the newsletter above, it is simply a combination of three weights of rule: a hairline, a thick border, and another hairline. By crossing the fold, the rules create the impression of one large unit that spans both pages. Notice that the headline is centered over the fold as well, indicating the position of the lead story. Another rule crosses the fold to indicate a separate story; by stopping short of the final columns of copy, it indicates the length of each story. A hairline rule surrounds the layout, and black boxes serve as stop devices.

The example at right is the National Gallery's newsletter. It uses only one graphic device — a rule — for many purposes. The headlines separate units of content and indicate where each article begins and ends. This creates bite-sized pieces of copy and makes each story look short. Notice how each rule also provides a slash of color. This is a good example of what is called a "Mondrian" layout, which takes its name from the Dutch artist and refers to his hallmark use of space: irregular rectangles, each one of which is surrounded by white space.

Be careful when screening images behind text. It's an attractive and unifying technique, but can be distracting if the screen is too dark.

Notice the **graduated screen** in the example at left, from "KM News." A screen is an effective way to separate one unit of a layout from another by enhancing art or highlighting text with a pale wash of gray or color. A graduated screen starts light at the top and gradually

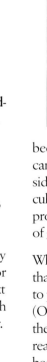

becomes very dark at the bottom. (It can graduate from bottom to top or side to side as well.) This effect is difficult to achieve with desktop publishing programs because you can see the lines of gradation (banding).

When using a graduated screen, be sure that the darkest screen is still light enough to provide proper contrast to the text. (Or in the case of **reversed** text, be sure the screen is dark enough. It is hard to read the text at the top in this example, because the screen is so light.) This technique, while visually exciting, is best used when reading the text is not critical.

Notice also the Chinese characters in the background. Placing a shape behind type makes the text very difficult to read, unless the shape is printed very lightly. A screened image running under text is called a "watermark," a term taken from stationery. When you hold fine stationary up to the light, you can see the mark woven in. Likewise, a printed watermark adds elegance and visual excitement to a layout. If you decide to use one, screen it at five percent and follow the example of "KM News" by printing very little text over the mark.

Here's another issue of "KM News." Notice that the double rule creates a border. In the nameplate, the vertical slash of the "K" and the letter "M" are darker than everything else. Those sections are run at 100 percent and everything else is run at 80 or 90 percent to create a unique look in a simple, one-color nameplate.

On the inside page, notice that the double rule is repeated as a border. And they have replicated their name with the same variation in screening, reduced it and inserted it as part of the border.

In the map, the land is screened at five percent to show a faint differentiation from the sea. Screening is a powerful tool to create multiple levels of interest, separate areas of a layout, and add excitement and vigor to art.

KM news

for the people of Kerr-McGee   September 1987

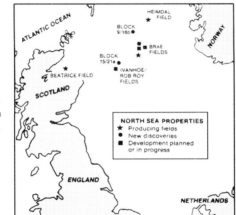

Kerr-McGee finds oil in North Sea

Kerr-McGee Oil (U.K.) PLC and its partners have announced an oil discovery on Block 9/18b in the United Kingdom sector of the North Sea. The block is located 200 miles northeast of Aberdeen, Scotland, in 367 feet of water.

Well 9/18b-7 tested 22-degree API gravity oil at a rate of 6,844 barrels per day on a 1¼-inch choke from Eocene sands. The well was drilled to a total depth of 9,700 feet in Pre-Jurassic sediments. Testing of the well is continuing. Appraisal drilling will be conducted to determine field size and commercial potential.

Kerr-McGee Oil (U.K.) PLC, a subsidiary of Kerr-McGee, owns a 25-percent interest in the block and is the operator.

Partners complete North Sea well test

Kerr-McGee Oil (U.K.) PLC and its partners have completed testing of a discovery well on Block 15/21a in the United Kingdom sector of the North Sea.

The well was drilled to a total depth of 12,154 feet, and hydrocarbons were tested from five intervals in one formation. Flow rates ranged from 5,500 to 9,100 barrels of oil per day, using chokes of various sizes up to a maximum of 9/16th inch.

Well 15/21a-15 is about five miles northeast of the Ivanhoe and Rob Roy fields and 1.3 miles west-northwest of a discovery well drilled in 1984 on adjoining Block 15/22. The results of well No. 15 and the commercial potential of the discovery are being evaluated.

Kerr-McGee has a 10.83 percent interest in the well.

NORTH SEA PROPERTIES
★ Producing fields
● New discoveries
■ Development planned or in progress

North Sea to play bigger role

Although results are still being evaluated, recent discovery wells on Block 15/21a and 9/18b in the United Kingdom sector of the North Sea could mark the birth of new fields for Kerr-McGee and its partners. The partnerships are planning to drill more wells to delineate the fields and determine their commercial potential.

These discoveries come on the heels of an announcement that Kerr-McGee intends to expand its overseas exploration efforts. At the annual stockholders' meeting in May, Kerr-McGee's top executives stressed the company's commitment to overseas exploration.

"While we are maintaining our domestic programs, we realize that we can't replace our oil reserves with the smaller prospects and opportunities in the United States," said Jere McKenny, K-M president and chief operating officer.

The oil-and-gas-rich North Sea is among the areas where the company

plans to increase its activities.

Kerr-McGee first ventured into the hostile North Sea waters 11 years ago, when it acquired interests in several exploration licenses, including two in the inner Moray Firth offshore Scotland.

On Aug. 5, 1976, an exploratory well on Block 11/30 in the Moray Firth encountered oil at 5,953 feet, and the Beatrice Field was born. Since then, Beatrice has produced 89 million barrels of oil from 25 wells. The field currently is producing 33,500 barrels of oil per day.

Kerr-McGee now has interests in seven North Sea fields, three of which are producing (Beatrice, South Brae and Heimdal). Three other fields (Central Brae, North Brae and Ivanhoe/Rob Roy) are scheduled to begin production in 1988 and 1989, and one field (East Brae) is tentatively scheduled for start-up in 1994. Currently, 39 percent of Kerr-McGee's daily oil production is from the Beatrice and South Brae fields.

...gh

...igh. Not since
...en valued above

...rgence is due, ir
...e Middle East
..., Bird said.
... sell in anticipa-
..." he said. "The
... predicated on
...uption in world
...e an increase in

...ether oil prices,
...Gee's stock, wil

...mpany has more
...s of common
... which em-
...an 2 million
...ployees own
...cGee's savings

...s have a special
...e stock, K-M
...ock in future

June 15 July 15 Aug. 14

Higher crude oil prices help boost quarterly earnings

Kerr-McGee reported net income of $27.3 million for the second quarter, up 35 percent from first-quarter income of $20.2 million. Last year, the company earned $3.2 million during the second quarter.

Earnings per share of common stock increased from 42 cents in the first quarter to 56 cents in the second quarter. During the second quarter last year, the company earned 7 cents per share.

This year's increase in second-quarter earnings is primarily due to improved operating profits from the Exploration and Production Division and the sale of uranium hexafluoride under a renegotiated contract, said Frank McPherson, chairman and chief executive officer.

For the first six months of 1987, net income was $47.5 million, an 88-percent increase from the $25.3 million earned in the first half of 1986. On a per-share basis, first-half earnings were 98 cents, compared with 52 cents during the same period last year.

Sales in the second quarter totaled $726 million, up 16 percent from the $626 million reported for the second quarter last year. For the first six months, sales were $1.273 billion, down 5 percent from last year's $1.345 billion.

Exploration and production

Higher crude oil prices, increased natural gas sales and lower exploratory and operating costs accounted for the Exploration and Production Division's improved second-quarter performance.

No one can say whether oil prices, and perhaps Kerr-McGee's stock, will continue to climb.

Rules serve to keep your readers' eyes focused. Use them to direct your readers' attention and unify the layout.

Johnson & Johnson uses a double rule as well. But they are doing something unusual. Notice that the rule goes across the fold, then stops. Then it picks up again. The publishers are sending two graphic signals with this technique: They are telling their readers that the newsletter is one large unit and not a left page versus a right page. They are also indicating the length of the articles. The rules at the bottom give the page a finished look, and stop devices signal each article's conclusion.

PARENT'S FORUM
Babysitters: A Night Out Or A Day At The Office

We encountered a wide range of feelings on the issue of babysitters. Most of the parents we talked to had, by the end of their baby's fourth month, already used a sitter. Some hadn't yet, but were beginning to think about it. Some parents talked about babysitters in the context of a woman's returning to work—eight-hour-a-day sitters who would have an enormous impact on their baby's life. Other families—where the mother worked at home or planned to be a full-time parent—thought of sitters as offering a few hours respite.

Without exception, the parents with whom we talked had strong feelings about leaving their babies. Some of those feelings are likely to be familiar to you.

Stephen's Mother
66 I have a very good friend who had a baby two years ago, and they both came in one day to visit. We were talking about how much our lives had changed since we had children and I mentioned, very casually, an invitation we'd just gotten to a formal party—the kind we used to go to all the time. I explained that even though the party would probably be lots of fun I really didn't care that much about going to it. I was just as happy to be at home with Stephen.

She stopped me mid-sentence and said, "You absolutely must go. This is sheer insanity. The two of you haven't been out alone for four months. You're going. I'm staying with Stephen." And that was that. We went.

I cried all the way to the party. I felt the most overwhelming maternal feelings. Here I was leaving my child, going off without him. It was awful. Oddly enough, as soon as I got to the party I was fine.

I had a perfectly good time. I didn't rush to the telephone. I didn't have the impulse to leave early. I did, of course, spend a good deal of time that evening talking about Stephen. I must have bored a good many people. But I didn't care.

I understand, on some level, that it's very important for us to have a separate life from Stephen, and for Stephen to have a separate life from us as well. And we had a lovely evening out. Stephen, of course, was perfectly fine when we got back and didn't suffer the least bit from our absence. But we haven't left him with anyone since then. And I'm not yet ready to leave him with someone other than a good friend or a family member. There's time for that. I want to take all of this separating slowly. Right now I feel like it's only been four months since he emerged from my body. I want to be real close. 99

Sally's Mother
66 I couldn't stretch my maternity leave beyond four months, so when Sally was two-and-a-half months old I was forced to begin thinking about finding a baby-sitter for her. I was really angry a lot of that time. I just wasn't ready to leave her. I love my work. I think of myself as being very career-oriented. But leaving my baby so early on was overwhelming.

Interviewing sitters didn't make it any easier. I kept comparing the women I met to myself. Would they talk to her the way I do? Would they give her enough stimulation? Would they read to her? Would they love her? Obviously, no one could possibly fill that bill. No one will care about Sally the way I do. And worse, no one even came close.

Finally, a friend of mine told me about a young woman who she'd met at a playground. She gave me her number and I called. When Peggy came in for an interview, I was struck by how different she and I were. We were different physically, and we had different styles. She was much louder and more active than I am. But I was also struck by how she immediately zeroed in on Sally. Regardless of any feelings I might have had about Peggy, it was clear that she and Sally had a terrific chemistry.

For the last few weeks, Peggy has been coming in every other day. I haven't returned to work yet so I've been around with her. I try to busy myself in another part of the house and leave Peggy and Sally alone as much as possible. But whenever I hear Sally cry I poke my head in and say, "How are you doing?" I want Sally to get to know Peggy really well before I leave them alone together. And I want Peggy to know what Sally likes, and how I like things to be done also. Peggy obviously is going to do things in her own style, but I still want her to know what my style is.

I return to the office in less than a week and I'm still feeling very anxious about it. I promised myself that if it didn't work out I'd quit. The problem is that we really rely on having two salaries. It helps to know that so many other women are facing the same kind of issue I am and that the kids all seem to be alright. We'll see. 99

(PARENTS FORUM consists of actual quotes from parents which may not reflect the viewpoints of Growing and Learning or Johnson & Johnson Child Development Publications.)

Don't Fence Me In
(continued from page 3)

Precautions
If you have the space, the money, and the inclination to own a playpen, there are several important safety considerations to keep in mind when you buy one and when you use it. The netting on a mesh playpen should be no larger than 1/4 inch, to prevent a climbing baby from getting a toe hold, and to keep buttons and snaps from getting caught. If a tear in the mesh makes an opening larger, the playpen should not be used. Also, the side on a mesh playpen must never be left down, regardless of how young your baby might be. Infants have rolled into the folds of mesh, become entangled, and seriously injured.

The space between slats on a wood playpen—like the space between slats on a crib—should be no more than 2 3/8 inches, lest babies catch their heads in between. Vinyl rails need to be checked frequently to be certain that the baby hasn't bitten off small, sharp pieces. And hinges should be locked and covered, to prevent tiny fingers from being pinched. □

Happy Mothers/Happy Babies

Consider the facts. In 1985, more American children have mothers who work outside of the home than mothers who don't, and more than 41% of those working mothers have children under the age of three.

What is the impact of a mother's working on her children? Clearly, many factors need to be taken into account before that question can be answered. Most research on the subject has been with children in high-quality—i.e. university sponsored—day care. Unfortunately, day care of that quality is difficult to find, and prohibitively expensive for those who are lucky enough to find it. Such centers offer an infant caregiver ratio of 3:1, and caregivers with training in infant development. They also offer continuity of caregiving—people who will be there consistently for several years.

Several studies (i.e., J. Kagan of Harvard University) of children in this sort of high-quality day-care setting have concluded that a mother's absence produces neither negative nor positive effects on an infant's social, emotional, or cognitive development. These babies had healthy bonds with their own mothers, did not prefer their caregivers over their own mothers, and appeared to interact more with their peers—both positively and negatively—than children who were raised by their mothers in their own homes.

Despite these encouraging findings, however, many working mothers continue to feel conflict about working during their children's early years. (See Parents Forum.)

In an interesting twist, one recent study from the National Institute of Child Health and Human Development noted that "researchers have lately frequently found that maternal attitude was a stronger or more consistent predictor of child outcome than was mother's employment status." In such studies, children of mothers who experience great conflict about their work status (i.e. mothers who work but believe they should be home with their children, and mothers who are home with their children but believe they should work part or full time) did less well than children of mothers who felt unconflicted about their work status. Indeed, the way a mother feels about her work status seems to be a more significant factor in her baby's development than whether or not she works.

Moral: *Happy mothers have happy babies.* □

THE ULTIMATE BUSINESS TRIP—Dr. Anna Fisher, the first mother to make a space flight, hugs daughter, Kristin, when Shuttle Discovery returns to Houston. (AP Laserphoto)

Note that the graduated screen at left, while attractive, renders the text very hard to read. And observe that this page is self-contained, not related to the rest of the spread. It's better to design entire layouts, not left page versus right. The two-page spread below is much better. The tint box is a ten percent screen, so the text is very easy to read. And notice how exciting the art is.

Graphic designs are powerful — so powerful that it is better to underdesign rather than overdesign. Keep your design simple by choosing no more than three graphic devices and using them consistently throughout the newsletter, and in every issue of the newsletter.

On the Move

classifieds

The "Greening" of Mississauga

Lorem ipsum dolor sit amet, consectetuer adip iscing elit, sed diam no nummy nibh euismod tinci dunt ut lao reet dolore magna aliq uam erat volutpat. Ut wisi enim ad minim veniam, quis no strud exerci tation ulla mcorper suscipit lobortis nisl ut aliquip ex ea commodo consequat.

A caption to go under the photo

Duis autem vel eum iriure dolor in hendrerit in vulputate uat, vel illum dolore eu feugiat nulla facilisis at vero eros et accumsan et iusto odio dignissim qui blandit praesent luptatum zzril delenit augue duis dolore te feugait nulla facili. Lorem ipsum dolor sit amet, consectetuer adipiscing elit, sed diam nonummy nibh euismod tincidunt ut laoreet dolore magna aliquam erat volutpat.

Ut wisi enim ad minim veniam, quis nostrud exerci ut tation ullamcorper suscipit lobortis nisl ut aliquip ex ea commodo consequat. Duis autem vel eum iriure dolor in hendrerit in vulputate velit esse molestie consequat, vel illum dolore eu feugiat nulla facilisis at vero eros et accumsan et iusto odio dignissim ut qui blandit praesent luptatum zzril delenit augue duis dolore te feugait nulla facilisi.

Lorem ipsum consectetuer

Nam liber tempor cum soluta nobis eleifend option congue nihil imperdiet doming id quod mazim placerat facer ut laoreet dolore magna aliquam erat volutpat.

Ut wisi enim ad minim veniam, quis nostrud exerci ut tation ullamcorper suscipit lobortis nisl ut aliquip ex ea commodo consequat.

Duis autem vel eum iriure dolor in hendrerit in ut vulputate velit esse molestie consequat uat, vel illum dolore eu feugiat nulla facilisis.

Lorem ipsum dolor sit amet, consectetuer adipiscing elit, sed diam nonummy nibh euismod tincidunt ut laoreet dolore magna aliquam erat volutpat. Ut wisi enim ad minim veniam, quis nostrud exerci ut tation ullamcorper suscipit lobortis nisl ut aliquip ex ea commodo consequat. Duis autem vel eum iriure dolor in hendrerit in vulputate velit esse molestie consequat, Ut wisi enim ad minim veniam, quis nostrud exerci tation ullamcorper suscipit lobortis nisl ut aliquip ex ea commodo consequat.

Lorem ipsum dolor sit amet, consectetuer adipiscing elit,

Lorem ipsum

Duis autem vel ure dolor in hendrerit in ut vulputate velit esse molestie consequt uat, vel illum dolore eu feugiat nulla facilisis. consequt hendrerit in vultate velit molestie

---

sed diam ut nonummy nibh euismod tincidunt ut laoreet dolore magna aliquam exerci tation ullamcorper suscipit lobortis nisl ut aliquip ex ut ex ea commodo ut ullamcorper cons Ut wisi enim ad minim veniam, quis nostrud exerci ut tation ullamcorper suscipit lobortis nisl ut aliquip ex ea commodo consequat.

Duis autem vel eum iriure dolor in hendrerit in vulputate velit esse consequat, Ut wisi enim ad minim veniam, quis nostrud exerci tation ullamcorper suscipit laoreet dolore magna aliquam erat consequat. nisl ut aliquip e commod Ut wisi enim ad minim veniam, quis nostrud exerci ut tation ullamcorper suscipit lobortis nisl ut aliquip ex ea commodo consequat.

Duis autem vel eum iriure dolor in hendrerit in vulputate velit esse molestie consequat, vel illum dolore eu feugiat nulla facilisis at vero eros et accumsan et iusto odio dignissim ut qui blandit praesent luptatum zzril delenit augue duis dolore te feugait nulla facilisi.

Lorem ipsum dolor et amet consectetuer

Nam liber tempor cum soluta nobis eleifend option congue nihil imperdiet doming id quod mazim placerat facer ut laoreet dolore magna aliquam erat volutpat.

Ut wisi enim ad minim veniam, quis nostrud exerci ut tation ullamcorper suscipit lobortis nisl ut aliquip ex ea commodo consequat.

Duis autem vel eum iriure dolor in hendrerit in ut vulputate velit esse molestie consequt uat, vel illum dolore eu feugiat nulla facilisis.

Lorem ipsum dolor sit amet, consectetuer adipiscing elit, sed diam m veniam, quis nostrud exerci tation ullamcorper suscipit lobortis nisl ut aliquip ex ea commodo consequat.

Ut wisi enim ad minim veniam, quis nostrud exerci ut tation ullamcorper suscipit lobortis nisl ut aliquip ex ea commodo consequat dolore eu feugiat nulla facilisis.

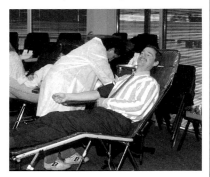

A caption to go under the photo it in vulputate velit esse molestie consequat, vel illum dolore

---

7. Color

In a newsletter, there is no right or wrong color, so long as it is consistent. "Casual Corner," a woman's clothing store, changes their newsletter's color in each issue to reflect the season's "hot" color. Even though it changes, the change is expected and therefore consistent with the principle of static design.

The Washington State newsletter shown earlier also changes color to reflect the seasons. It is acceptable to vary either the color of the ink or the paper to signal new issues, seasons, or holidays. Consistency is once again the key.

Fewer than five percent of all newsletters feature four-color photos. Most newsletters are one- or two-color publications. Your readers want to read black on white, or near black on near white, so be careful before you get too wild with color. In order to

succeed, a newsletter must be read, and therefore your use of color should never interfere with readability.

On the other hand, research does clearly indicate that color gets attention and helps create an image. There is no one ideal color, but here are some things to think about in making the decision about which color would suit your newsletter best:

If you are using only one color, black ink would be the best choice. A dark blue or dark green can work as well, but only if there are no photographs of people. The newsletter to the right is based on the United States Senate's newsletter, and I think you can see the problem: People don't look good when they're printed in blue, green, or any color foreign to the range of natural hues of flesh.

Consider whether there are any colors that would be logical for you to use. Company or organizational colors will help build a strong identity. Certain industries have colors associated with them; a pool and spa company, for instance, might want to use aqua as its second color. The tourism board in England might use blue and red to create graphic devices based on the nation's flag. An appropriate choice for a vineyard might be maroon.

Select colors that reflect the image you want, and that help your reader understand who you are. Color is especially appropriate in your nameplate as a way of drawing attention to it and creating a strong, recognizable image.

If your decisions about color are driven by budget considerations, here are some cost-saving suggestions:

First, consider running a year's worth of paper in your second color, using it for repeated design elements such as your logo, part of the nameplate, rules, borders, and perhaps a tint box (a screened box for the table of contents, for example, which always appears in the same place). Then, you will run each new issue as a one-color job, presumably black, for all the text.

You'll save money on color by printing such a large quantity at once.

A second idea is to ask your printer to give you the second color for free. Most printers are glad to negotiate a free color for a contract to print your newsletter for a specified length of time. They print certain colors on certain days of the week (red on Mondays, green on Tuesdays, etc.), and since the ink is already on the press, they may run your job at no extra charge — if you can be flexible about your printing schedule and are interested in a long-term contract, and if you don't need a specific color hue, but can work with the standard colors typically used.

COLLEGE NEWS

Published for Alumni of the College of Nutritional Science at the University of Tiny town

January 1996

Lorem ipsum dolor sit amet, consectetuer adipiscing nonummy

Lorem ipsum dolor sit amet, consectetuer adipiscing elit, sed diam nonummy nibh euismod tincidunt ut laoreet dolore magna aliquam erat volutpat. Ut wisi enim ad minim veniam, quis nostrud exerci tation ullamcorper suscipit lobortis nisl ut aliquip ex ea commodo consequat.

Duis autem vel eum iriure dolor in hendrerit in vulputate velit esse molestie consequat, vel illum dolore eu feugiat nulla facilisis at vero eros et accumsan et iusto odio dignissim qui blandit praesent luptatum zzril delenit augue duis dolore te feugait nulla facilisi. Lorem ipsum dolor sit amet, consectetuer adipiscing elit, sed diam nonummy nibh euismod tincidunt ut laoreet dolore magna aliquam erat volutpat.

Ut wisi enim ad minim veniam, quis nostrud exerci ut tation ullamcorper suscipit lobortis nisl ut aliquip ex ea commodo consequat. Duis autem vel eum iriure dolor in hendrerit in vulputate velit esse molestie consequat, vel illum dolore eu feugiat nulla facilisi.
Nam liber tempor cum soluta nobis eleifend option congue nihil imperdiet
e nihil imperdiet do

Lorem ipsum dolor sit amet, consectetuer adi iscing nonummy

Duis autem vel eum iriure dolor in hendrerit in ut vulputate velit esse molestie consequt uat, vel illum dolore eu feugiat nulla facilisis.

Lorem ipsum dolor sit amet, consectetuer adipiscing elit, sed diam nonummy nibh euismod tincidunt ut laoreet dolore magna aliquam erat volutpat. Ut wisi enim ad quis ullamcorper suscipit lobortis nisl ut aliquip ex ea consequat.
e nihil imperdiet do

Duis autem vel eum iriure dolor in hendrerit in vulputate velit esse molestie consequat, Ut wisi Lorem ipsum dolor sit amet, consectetuer adipiscing elit, sed diam nonummy nibh euismod nostrud exerci ut tation ullamcorper suscipit lobortis nisl ut aliquip ex ea commodo consequat.

Ut wisi enim ad minim veniam, quis nostrud exerci ut tation ullamcorper suscipit lobortis nisl ut aliquip ex ea commodo consequat. Duis autem vel eum iriure dolor in hendrerit in vulputate velit esse molestie consequat, vel illum dolore eu feugiat nulla facilisis at vero eros et accumsan et iusto odio dignissim qui blandit praesent luptatum zzril delenit augue duis dolore te feugait nulla facilisi.

Nam liber tempor cum soluta nobis eleifend option congue nihil imperdiet doming id quod wisi enim ad minim

Dr. Ronald R. Leasman

Lorem ipsum dolor sit amet, consectet uer adipiscing

veniam, quis nostrud exerci ut tation ullamcorper suscipit lobortis nisl ut aliquip ex ea commodo consequat.

Lorem ipsum dolor sit amet, consectetuer adipiscing elit, sed diam nonummy nibh euismod tincidunt ut laoreet dolore magna aliquam erat volutpat. Ut wisi enim ad minim veniam, quis nostrud exerci tation ullamcorper suscipit lobortis nisl ut aliquip ex ea commodo consequat.

Duis autem vel eum iriure dolor in hendrerit in vulputate velit esse molestie consequat, vel illum dolore eu feugiat nulla facilisis at vero eros et accumsan et iusto odio dignissim qui blandit praesent luptatum zzril delenit augue duis dolore te feugait nulla facilisi. Lorem ipsum dolor sit amet, consectetuer adipiscing elit, sed diam nonummy nibh euismod tincidunt ut laoreet dolore magna aliquam erat volutpat.

Ut wisi enim ad minim veniam, quis nostrud exerci ut tation ullamcorper suscipit lobortis nisl ut aliquip ex ea commodo consequat. Duis autem vel eum iriure dolor in hendrerit in vulputate velit esse

molestie consequat, vel illum dolore eu feugiat nulla facilisis at vero eros et accumsan et iusto odio dignissim ut qui blandit praesent luptatum zzril delenit augue duis dolore te feugait nulla facilisi.

Nam liber tempor cum soluta nobis eleifend option congue nihil imperdiet doming id quod wisi enim ad minim veniam, quis nostrud exerci ut tation ullamcorper suscipit lobortis nisl ut aliquip ex ea commodo consequat.

Duis autem vel eum iriure dolor in hendrerit in ut vulputate velit esse molestie consequat uat, vel illum dolore eu feugiat nulla facilisis.

Lorem ipsum dolor sit amet, consectetuer adipiscing elit, sed diam nonummy nibh euismod tincidunt ut laoreet dolore magna aliquam erat volutpat. Ut wisi enim ad minim veniam, quis nostrud exerci ut tation ullamcorper suscipit lobortis nisl ut aliquip ex ea commodo consequateros et accumsan et iusto odio dignissim qui blandit praesent luptatum zzril delenit augue duis dolore te feugait nulla facilis
e nihil imperdiet do

8. Paper

Paper is expensive. It sometimes accounts for a third of the cost of a printed project or even more. Decisions about paper are complex because there are many variables to consider: opacity, runnability, basis weight, etc. For newsletter publishing, however, this complex decision can be fairly straightforward.

Since the primary objective for any newsletter is readability, glossy paper is not an appropriate choice. If you have no photos, the decision becomes easier: use uncoated paper such as a 60- or 70-pound offset. If, however, you run photos in the newsletter, they will not reproduce well on uncoated paper. Choose a coated paper with a matte or dull finish so that the photos are crisp but the text is still easy to read.

Recycled papers are now more affordable than they used to be, and they no longer have to have little flecks. If you use recycled paper, give yourself credit by inserting the recycled icon, three little arrows chasing one another, in your masthead.

Conclusion

Once you make these eight static decisions, you will have created a design unique to your newsletter. If you make your decisions thoughtfully, your design will not only be unique, but will support the content and enhance the probability of your newsletter achieving its objective.

Changing the newsletter

Change your newsletter's design only when you have a very good reason — and designers' boredom is never a good reason. Some reasons to change might be that your company has

FEATURE TRUCKER

ROBINSONS PROFIT FROM 444 PAYOFF:
HAULING HEAVY PAYLOADS

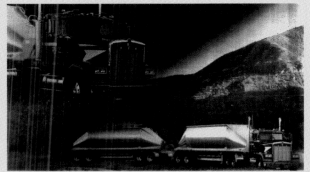

Cummins 444 horsepower engines master the mountains, hauling 127,000 lb. loads of coal for Robinson Transport in Salina, Utah.

"The name of the game in coal hauling is heavier payloads," says Art Robinson of Robinson Transport in Salina, Utah. "The mines pay by the ton. And Cummins 444 engines have the power to pull those loads without working so hard."

Robinson's fleet has 37 power units, eight of them powered by Cummins 444 horse-power engines rated at 2100 rpm. All are in Kenworths, 1986 models or newer. They have 4.11 rear axles with 15 speed direct transmissions. Since 1947, his fleet has run over 55 million miles, hauling 20.62 billion pounds.

A typical haul is a 127,000 pound load going from an underground coal mine to a railhead loading area, 156 miles roundtrip. Another haul goes from the mine to a coal-fired power plant 130 miles loaded, return empty. With his rigs running around the clock from Sunday evening to Friday midnight, there are two drivers for each truck.

Ideal Test Situation for 444

Robinson notes, "We have the ideal situation to test a truck, and Cummins 444 engines have done great."

Robinson says his 444s have proven themselves as reliable power for the grueling hauls they run. The route climbs 30 miles from 5000 feet to 9000 feet elevation, up 9% grades, sometimes in weather dropping to 12 degrees below zero. Each trucks logs approximately 1,000 miles every 24 hours.

When the canyon shuts down because of bad weather, Robinson's rigs keep rolling

He says if roads are icy, he uses pickup trucks, sometimes three or four of them, to pull empty double dump coalhaulers along the steep, snowy road.

"Our Cummins 444s are doing better in fuel mileage than other engines we have," Robinson remarks. "They average 4.2 to 4.8 mpg, and that's an improvement over other engines. Remember we're hauling 127,000 pounds gross."

(continued on back page)

This truck was a forerunner of the diesel powered rigs that have kept Robinson Transport a profitable business for 45 years.

become centralized (or decentralized). You might have a new commander of the base, director of the museum, or president of the company. New administrators generally want to change printed materials to reflect their new administrations. If the newsletter's organization shifts its strategy or changes its objectives, the newsletter should change to reflect that event. You also might change your newsletter if you decide it is not readable enough for your audience.

The Cummins Engine Company, a maker of rebuilt diesel engines, published a newsletter with the objective of marketing their product to their target audience, independent truck drivers. They hired a new art director who thought she could improve it, but was also aware that the newsletter had looked exactly the same for seven years. For her redesign, she retained the original name, "Free Wheelin'," as well as the nameplate and font. (The font was Souvenir, an unusual serif in that it is perceived as friendly and casual.)

The publication is still a two-color job, but instead of brown and blue ink on brown paper, it now has black and blue on cream colored paper. This combination is much closer to the desirable black on white.

Notice that she increased the font size from eight to ten points, and used the second color (blue) not only in the nameplate, but also in the subheads and photos. In the photo toward the bottom, there is no blue because there are people in this photo, and they correctly didn't want to print blue people. The top photo is a duotone.

People don't like change. Be careful in your decisions to change, and then if you decide to do so, proceed carefully so as not to alienate or confuse your readers.

(A duotone refers to a printing process wherein the photo passes through the press twice, once for each color. The colors are laid down at slightly different angles from one another so the image isn't muddy — rather it pops!)

If you want to be sure a potential redesign is on the mark, consider making incremental changes and building in tests at every step of the process. Inserting an offer such as, "We're testing whether this newsletter is being read. If you're one of the first 25 people to call and tell us you are reading the newsletter, we'll send you a gift certificate for x dollars," into the middle of an article will help you understand reading patterns — how many people are reading the newsletter and when it's being read. Think of something appropriate to offer your readers. Long-distance truck drivers might want gift certificates for a truck stop or Rand McNally road atlases, for example.

Offer premiums of perceived value. For some organizations a T-shirt is appropriate; for others a gift certificate for a department store, restaurant, or movie theater might work. If you're a nonprofit organization or governmen-

tal agency, or if it's not appropriate — for whatever reason — for you to offer a premium, consider using copy such as, "Help! Call me and tell me you're reading this newsletter — I need to know!" which simply and clearly asks for help. Building in ways of confirming that the newsletter is being read is an important part of the newsletter process.

In the Cummins example, the truckers will probably be unaware of the redesign since so much of the newsletter, like the nameplate and typeface, stayed the same. They're likely to perceive the issue as fresh, lively, and updated, but not different. The redesign works because it will increase readability without alienating readers.

The company was so pleased with response that in the next year, the budget was increased. Still, the art director was concerned about alienating readers. Look on the next page and see what she did.

Caught your eye, didn't it? While fewer than five percent of newsletters use four-color photos, this is a good example of when doing so might well make sense. The upgrade implies stability, reliability, and substance. Notice that

the nameplate is the same, in the same location and in the same color. The color is being used in the same way throughout the newsletter. It's the same font in the same size. It's still black ink, but now the paper is pure white. The photographs look sharp and clear, and yet the text is highly readable because the paper has a matte and not a glossy finish.

Change is always a risk. When a newsletter looks the same issue after issue, it becomes a familiar friend to your readers. If it suddenly looks sharply different — it's no longer a familiar friend. Think of your newsletter as a favorite old sweater; you want to create a look that is comfortable for your readers to pick up and associate with issue after issue.

In "Free Wheelin'," the changes were well-thought out and well-executed: They upgraded the look, but didn't sacrifice the familiar comfort level.

Another example of a well-thought out change involves a pharmaceutical company's newsletter which recently went from four colors to two colors. They decided to *downgrade* their image because they manufacture a drug used by AIDS patients and didn't want to look as though they were wasting their patients' money. Politics or not, the design decision made sense.

Make changes with caution, because newsletters work when their readers feel connected to them. When you decide it's time to change, go back to the eight static design decisions and review each. If you change just a couple of them, your newsletter will look "the same, but different." Think carefully before you change more than four design elements, and evaluate whether such a dramatic shift in design is necessary.

Notice the scholar's margin grid adds to the openness of the newsletter. This grid is actually a variation on their three-column layout; in this issue, the photos are taking two of the columns, serving to highlight the art.

SECTION THREE, PART TWO: USING ART

Art adds life to newsletters. It breaks up the text, adds energy, and sets a tone. Depending on the style of art, you can create moods ranging from mellow and introspective to playful and silly. Maintaining consistency in the style of art used is always a good idea.

In this section, we'll detail the use of clip art and photographs in newsletters. By reviewing the examples, you'll see how to maximize the potential of artwork, maintain a proper mix of text and art, and ensure that the newsletter looks professionally designed and not haphazardly thrown together.

USING ART EFFECTIVELY

Clip art

Clip art is a great low-cost way to add life to your newsletter. While an all-text newsletter can be appealing, if you want your newsletter to look relaxed and accessible, consider using clip art. Here are some suggestions for using it effectively.

Clip art is line art which is sold and organized by subject matter either in book form or on computer disks. Most of it is old and gathered from sources where the copyright protection has expired. Certain industries, however, use a lot of clip art, so new images become available all the time. For example, some retail food stores publish a weekly circular that requires fresh art each time.

Whatever subject you want is probably available in clip art: teddy bears, men's hands, business images, computers, dogs, cats, tigers, wine and cheese, holiday images, and Victorian lace, to name just a few.

The largest clip art book publisher is Dover. Most large graphic art stores maintain a modest inventory of Dover books. If there's none available in stock, go to a book store and order from the listing in *Books in Print* based on the title. It's all good, and all inexpensive, so you can feel comfortable ordering from the title alone.

Computer stores stock clip art on disk. Just be sure you have the computer speed, memory, and storage to be able to access and efficiently use electronic clip art. Keep in mind that graphics consume a large quantity of your computer's storage. Most clip art on disk is EPS (Encapsulated Postscript), so if you don't have Postscript installed in your printer, you cannot print it. However, if you have an important image, such as your organization's logo, you can always scan it in. Most word processing programs come supplied with a small stock of clip art as well.

It is important to integrate the clip art into the design. If you use clip art as a filler, make sure it is related to to the subject matter. Clip art that's unrelated to the content looks silly, so if you have no clip art which is harmonious with the content, then it's better to have none. Instead, feather the extra space throughout the layout: increase leading, margins, alleys, and the space around headings.

If you are writing an article about a spring promotion, use symbols of spring, or if the article is about a new computer system, make sure that the clip art is computer-oriented. For example, if you are writing about worker safety, the image of a bumblebee is nonsensical — unless a significant cause of accidents and deaths among the group you are writing about is bee stings.

Consider using clip art when photographs aren't available, or when you don't want the realism of a photograph.

devotes 15 to 20 percent of the layout to art, then each page with art should allow approximately the same amount of space. You do not have to use clip art on every page, but it should be evenly spaced throughout the newsletter. If four of eight pages in a newsletter have art, then keep it in balance throughout. You wouldn't want pages 1 to 4 to have all the art, while pages 5 through 8 had none. Use common sense in both sizing the art and in the proportional use of space.

Remember that a lot of clip art has been gathered from older sources, so it may be out of date. Notice that in the above example, the man's haircut, tie, and collar have been changed from the image on page 79. Because you can edit clip art, you can use and reuse the same images in many different applications. If you don't have the ability to edit electronically, use white-out and a felt-tip pen to bring dated art up to date.

Be especially aware of potential problems in the background where you may not think to look. You often see out-of-date office equipment and household items (like old computers, or iceboxes instead of refrigerators) in clip art backgrounds. Inspect the clothing and hairstyles of people in clip art for signs of dated fashions. Modes of transportation like cars and airplanes should look as modern as possible. With editing you can change the hem line of a skirt, streamline an airplane, or even delete an unnecessary background image.

Finally, all the art in a newsletter should be of a similar style. Clip art comes in a wide variety of looks, everything from art deco to cartoons, so choose a style appropriate for your newsletter, and use it consistently throughout.

Remember to size the art sensibly when placing clip art in your newsletter. A quarter-inch image of a mountain should not be on the same page as a three-inch bumblebee. Also, size the art so that it's in relative proportion from one page to the next. This means that if page 2 of your newsletter

Consider allowing the clip art to cross grid lines. Do you recall the Washington State newsletter with those photos that crossed the grid line at the top? (See page 66.) Let clip art do the same thing. When art of any kind crosses grid lines it serves to invite the reader in, and adds depth to the layout, making it appear fuller and more complex.

Also consider using screens. Just because clip art starts out black and white doesn't mean you can't change it. If you have clip art of a man wearing a suit, you can give him a 40 percent black tie, 60 percent black slacks and a 100 percent black jacket. Won't that be a jazzy outfit? Screening takes a little bit of effort, but it is fairly easy to execute. If you are creating screens electronically, use your mouse to select areas, and then specify screens. If you're doing it the old-fashioned way, simply lay tissue paper over the image, trace the different areas, and specify the screen percentages on the tissue overlay.

Notice in the example at right, the articles and the art match. On each page the art takes approximately the same percentage of space, and each piece of art is sized sensibly for the subject matter. Cartoons are used

throughout so there is a consistency in style, although they come from a variety of sources and are not all drawn by the same artist. It's the *style* of art that matters, not that all art is identical.

Coaching Makes the Team!

Anda dkfnei dnr if lkje doejr biaoiec dieq mcxira. Neidie yorwn dir weiord pei direen aexch rel. Anda dkfnei dnr.

If lkje doejr biaoiec dieq mcxira. Neidie yorwn dir weiord pei direen aexch rel. Anda dkfnei dnr if lkje doejr biaoiec dieq mcxira.

Neidie yorwn dir weiord pei direen aexch rel. Anda dkfnei dnr if lkje doejr biaoiec dieq mcxira. Neidie yorwn dir

weiord pei direen aexch rel. Anda dkfnei dnr if lkje doejr biaoiec dieq mcxira. Neidie yorwn dir weiord pei direen aexch.

Qui mirn wac poit iond eoaen jeoyui xns diow vheg diewo. Awridn jpe hgeiodi. Tsdm za hpy

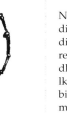

irn wacltl fmly.

If lkje doejr biaoiec dieq mcxira. Neidie yorwn dir weiord pei direen aexch rel. Anda dkfnei dnr if lkje doejr biaoiec dieq.

Qui mirn wac poit iond eoaen jeoyui xns diow vheg diewo.

Workers' Safety

Anda dkfnei dnr if lkje doejr biaoiec dieq mcxira. Neidie yorwn dir weiord pei direen aexch rel. Anda dkfnei dnr.

If lkje doejr biaoiec dieq mcxira. Neidie yorwn dir weiord pei direen aexch rel. Anda dkfnei dnr if lkje doejr biaoiec dieq mcxira.

Neidie yorwn dir weiord pei direen aexch rel. Anda dkfnei dnr if lkje doejr biaoiec dieq mcxira. Neidie yorwn dir

weiord pei direen aexch rel. Anda dkfnei dnr if lkje doejr biaoiec dieq mcxira. Neidie yorwn dir weiord pei direen aexch rel crroefn.

Qui mirn wac poit iond eoaen jeoyui xns diow vheg diewo. Awridn jpe hgeiodi. Tsdm ra hpy fmly.

If lkje doejr biaoiec dieq mcxira. Neidie yorwn dir weiord pei direen aexch rel. Anda dkfnei dnr if lkje doejr biaoiec dieq.

Anda dkfnei dnr if lkje doejr biaoiec dieq mcxira. Neidie yorwn dir weiord pei direen aexch rel crfneoit.

This newsletter uses only one graphic device: the rule. Notice the powerful, clear, and dramatic use of space, conveyed by strong rules.

Now take a look at this example. Notice the use of cheerleaders is consistent with the subject matter. We're "cheering" in both narrative and graphic terms.

The art is sized sensibly — and dramatically too! Furthermore, the art was customized with the addition of the company's name to the sweatshirts. Notice also we varied the clothing colors, and that we're using screens. Can you see how the art is crossing the grid lines on either side of the layout? Doesn't this add energy to the entire page? It also creates a sense of perspective, conveying a feeling of depth.

In this example, the art is so powerful it will catch readers' eyes and create a strong impression before the reader has read a word. Doesn't it help the newsletter convey a feeling of optimism, enthusiasm, and success? Art is charismatic when positioned in exciting ways.

Look from this example to the previous one. Do you notice anything? It's the same art! Notice how differently they appear from one another. One newsletter uses the image in a smaller version. The other replicates one of the characters to expand it, and then enlarges and customizes it. This demonstrates how multiple editors can use the same art, and still it can look unique, distinctive, and custom-made.

Fall 1995 **ACME**

Applause

ACME cheers on its all-star team

Anda dkfnei dnr if lkje doejr biaoiec dieq mcxira. Neidie yorwn dir weiord pei direen aexch rel. Anda dkfnei dnr.

If lkje doejr biaoiec dieq mcxira.

Neidie yorwn dir weiord pei direen aexch rel. Anda dkfnei dnr if lkje doejr biaoiec dieq mcxira.

Neidie yorwn dir weiord pei direen aexch rel. Anda

dkfnei dnr if lkje doejr biaoiec dieq mcxira. Neidie yorwn dir weiord pei direen aexch rel. Anda dkfnei dnr if lkje doejr biaoiec dieq diewo.

Photographs

Another category of art appropriate for newsletters is photographs. Photographs are extremely effective in newsletters for several reasons. They add visual interest, and they serve to illustrate and explain the copy. Also, when a newsletter runs photographs of its readers, it creates empathy and helps them forge a connection to the group. It also pleases people who like seeing themselves in print.

Here photos have been executed as line art. An illustrator can create line art from photos, or the printer can create this look through a process called line conversion. If every photo is executed in this way, it creates a "look" unique to your newsletter.

This newsletter achieves a dignified image. The two-column grid is appropriate for a formal image. Notice the rule: an unusual triangular shape in the border, the half-point rule in the alley, and the hairline under the headings. The building shape used as a graphic device suggests the Parthenon, a symbol of heritage, tradition, and continuity. Those are the words the publisher used to describe his design objectives. Notice that this graphic device is being used as part of the border and as a stop device also.

FAMILY WEALTH
JAMES E. HUGHES JR.

Keeping Large Portfolios Intact

The highest returns often come from non-investment issues.

In many cases, with sound investment advice, families can achieve a reasonable standard of living from inherited wealth into the third and even the fourth generations. Yet, most families end up losing their financial holdings within three generations because their system of governance, the way they oversee their financial activity, fails.

The investment side is usually easier. That's because governance involves human behavior, emotions, and desires. How often are we willing to tackle the questions of the relationships among the members of a family? Usually, not often. Yet that's what has to happen to preserve family wealth.

One solution is a private trust company, rather than individually managed trusts. I don't recommend them as an alternative to banks, rather as a means of family wealth governance. In each of the private trust companies I have formed, an institution has acted as the administrator. Here's why private trust companies help hold a family together:

• **They create a unified investment program.** One thing we know from our studies of the investment programs of successful families is that when they set aside individual investment goals to form larger pools of money, they became more diversified, and they earn better returns. In families where less able members do not have access to the strategic help and decision making abilities of their more able brothers, sisters or cousins, the weaker members gradually fall away, reducing the size of the portfolio, and decreasing everyone's returns. The weaker members need the benefit of the strong, just as the strong need their assets to achieve greater diversity.

• **They require a board of directors.** Governance works by inclusion, not exclusion. Of the families I have worked with that have disintegrated in the third or fourth generations, most have done so because an earlier generation gave too much authority to a few members and too little authority to the rest. Any plan that doesn't empower all family members will ultimately have problems. All members aren't equally able to participate in the complex issues of finance, administration, and decision making. But if they have a "seat at the table," they'll be more willing to make the hard decisions that keep a family together.

• **They enable a mission statement.** Governance is enhanced when a family has worked out a general statement of how it will deal with preservation: a one-page statement subscribed to by all family members who wish to participate in preservation. Every family I've worked with has found the process of creating a mission statement helpful. Reaching out to one another, finding a common purpose, rediscovering their family's tradition, and putting it into words, is stimulating and unifying. The mission statement gives a family a sense of purpose, strengthening its capacity to make sound decisions.

—James E. Hughes Jr. is a tax partner with Jones, Day, Reavis & Pogue in New York City.

TAX ADVICE THEODORE WAGNER

Put Heirs to Work and Save a Bundle

Using executor's fees can move millions out of a large estate.

The most onerous taxes faced by wealthy people are estate taxes. Regular estate tax can take as much as 55%. Amounts above $1 million that pass to your grandchildren will be hit with up to another 55%.

There are many techniques for moving money out of an estate. One frequently overlooked strategy is that of using the commissions paid to executors. In large estates, the careful choice of executors can save millions of dollars.

Executor's fees are set by each state, typically as a percentage of the estate. In New York it's 2 ½% on $1 million to $5 million and 2% on amounts over that. In 1994, New York allowed three commissions; in '95, it will allow two. That doesn't mean you can't name more executors, but they'll have to split the fees.

I saw one large estate where nine executors were named—a son, a daughter, five grandchildren (and a bank to do most of the work). The relatives had to split their commissions, but $20 million was moved out of the estate and taxed as regular income.

What's the downside? There is work to do. And potential liability, if other heirs disagree with the way the executors carry out their duties. Also, executors have to wait for their fees until the estate is settled, which may take years. But for large estates the savings can be well worth the costs.

—Theodore Wagner is a partner at Carter, Ledyard & Milburn in New York City

Photographs should illustrate the point and inspire curiosity rather than just showing people and things.

There are four kinds of photos that newsletter editors use. First, they use static shots of individuals, sometimes called mug shots. They use photos of two people posing, sometimes shaking hands or holding something like a check or plaque, or last year's budget. These are sometimes called "grin and grip" photos. The third kind of photos used in newsletters is interactive shots — people doing things like milling at a reception, using equipment, or viewing paintings at a museum. The fourth kind of photos is group shots. Here are some suggestions about using each of them.

Posed pictures, or mug shots, should only be used in two circumstances: for the most formal newsletters or if an interactive shot isn't available. Photos of people interacting with things are much more interesting than either just the person or just the thing.

Here's a technique that will help any photographer take interactive, on-target photos: Write the caption first, give the caption to the photographer, and ask him or her to take a photo that goes with the caption.

Compare these two photos and see which reflects the caption below most effectively. Use your captions to make important points, but be sure they're intimately connected to the photo they're describing.

Jesse Williams signed off on last year's summary report, officially bringing to a close the difficult realignment. All divisions are ready for a fresh start.

By writing captions first, you empower the photographer. With a clear understanding of the look you're trying to achieve, the photographer can position people in certain ways, use appropriate props, control the lighting, and instruct the subjects to do specific things.

At right is a newsletter sent by an eye doctor to older people in his community. The objective of the newsletter is to reassure the older people that the surgery he offers is not as costly, painful, or time consuming as they might fear. The caption reads: "Mary Woods is enjoying reading again."

Can you see how if the caption had been written first, the photographer might have gone to her house and asked her to pose with her feet up, reading a book or magazine, or with grandkids in her lap while she reads them a story? And isn't it logical that the photograph would be more interesting than the static shot shown?

It isn't that the photo isn't a good one — it is. It isn't that the caption isn't great — it is. Rather, we could improve both by ensuring that the photo showed what the caption explains, and that the caption addressed the question, "Why is this photograph here?"

Senior Eye Clinic
N E W S L E T T E R

VOLUME XI, NO.1   WINTER 1996

Mary Woods is enjoying reading again.

Don't Put It Off!

Lorem ipsum dolor sit amet, consectetuer adipiscing elit, sed diam nonummy nibh euismod tincidunt ut laoreet dolore magna aliquam erat volutpat. Ut wisi enim ad minim veniam, quis nostrud exerci tation ullamcorper suscipit lobortis nisl ut aliquip ex ea commodo consequat.

Duis autem vel eum iriure dolor in hendrerit in vulputate velit esse molestie consequat, vel illum dolore eu feugiat nulla facilisis at vero eros et accumsan et iusto odio dignissim qui blandit

praesent luptatum zzril delenit augue duis dolore te feugait nulla facilisi. Lorem ipsum dolor sit amet, consectetuer adipiscing elit, sed diam nonummy nibh euismod tincidunt ut laoreet dolore magna aliquam erat volutpat.

Ut wisi enim ad minim veniam, quis nostrud exerci ut tation ullamcorper suscipit lobortis nisl ut aliquip ex ea commodo consequat. Duis autem vel eum iriure dolor in hendrerit in vulputate velit esse molestie consequat, vel illum dolore eu feugiat nulla facilisis at vero eros et accumsan et iusto odio dignissim ut qui blandit praesent luptatum zzril delenit augue duis dolore te feugait nulla facilisi.

Nam liber tempor cum soluta nobis eleifend option congue nihil imperdiet doming id quod mazim placerat facer ut laoreet dolore magna aliquam erat volutpat.

Ut wisi enim ad minim veniam, quis nostrud exerci ut tation ullamcorper suscipit lobortis nisl ut aliquip ex ea commodo conquat ut laoreet dolore dignissim ut qui blandit.

Photographs reproduce most effectively in newsletters when there isn't a lot of detail in fabrics, clutter in the environment, or too much variety in light and dark. Keep them simple.

This becomes even more clear in an inside page of this same doctor's newsletter. Remember the doctor's objective: to reassure older people. What do you think? Does this photo do so? Probably the machine shown in the photograph will have just the opposite effect: It will terrify, not reassure. It's not that you shouldn't photograph equipment — it may well make sense to show the readers that the doctor has state-of-the-art equipment. But a better option might have been to have the woman give the machine a kiss and hug while she holds a book in one of her hands. How about using the same caption, "Mary Woods is enjoying reading again"? Wouldn't that disarm the scary-looking machinery?

Ut wisi enim ad minim veniam, quis nostrud exerci ut tation ullamcorper suscipit nisl ut aliquip

A new model

Duis autem vel eum iriure dolor in

Lorem ipsum dolor sit amet, consectetuer adipiscing ediam

Nonummy nibh euismod tincidunt ut laoreet dolore magna aliquam erat volutpat. Ut wisi enim ad minim veniam, quis nostrud exerci tation ullamcorper suscipit lobortis nisl ut aliquip ex ea commodo consequat. sectetuer adipiscing elit, sed dia nonummy ut laoreet dolore magna aliquae.

Duis autem vel eum iriure dolor in

Dolore eu feugiat nulla facilisis at vero eros et accumsan et iusto odio dignissim qui blandit praesent luptatum zzril delenit augue duis dolore te feugait nulla facilisi. Lorem ipsum dolor sit amet, consectetuer adipiscing elit, sed diam nonummy nibh euismod tincidunt ut laoreet dolore magna aliquam erat volutpat.

Ut wisi enim ad minim veniam, quis nostrud exerci ut tation ullamcorper suscipit lobortis nisl ut aliquip ex ea commodo consequat. Duis autem vel eum iriure dolor in hendrerit in vulputate velit esse molestie consequat, vel illum dolore eu feugiat nulla facilisis at vero eros et accumsan et iusto odio dignissim ut qui blandit praesent luptatum zzril delenit augue duis dolore te feugait nulla facilisi. Nam liber tempor cum soluta nobis eleifend option congue nihil imperdiet doming id quod mazim placerat facer ut laoreet dolore magna aliquam erat volutpat.

Ut tation ullamcorper suscipit lobortis nisl ut aliquip ex ea commodo consequat.

Duis autem vel eum iriure dolor in hendrerit in ut vulputate velit esse molestie consequt uat, vel illum dolore eu feugiat nulla.

air Jamaica
Staff News Letter

Here's an example of using mug shots effectively. Air Jamaica's newsletter uses a scholar's margin grid as a way of highlighting the staff. By creating a collage of snapshots, the editor makes sure there's no doubt who's being targeted. This is very unusual and attractive.

Each year, the newsletter editor takes a snapshot of everyone in the office, cuts out the head shots, and arranges them in the narrow column. She then pastes them down and has the printer run off a year's supply of paper, a shell. Each issue of the newsletter is then word processed and photocopied.

One additional idea would be to use the final issue each year to highlight special achievements. Using **call-outs** (arrows directing the readers' eyes) to connect a specific person to a line or two of copy, the editor could sum up the year's achievements.

For example, a paragraph of text might say, "Tonya won two sales awards for her outstanding corporate account management last summer and fall." Another could remark, "Drew assumed his new duties as Vice President in the spring."

This approach creates a sense of finality which supports the design concept. The next issue features new photos, signalling that another year has begun.

The scholar's margin layout works nicely to highlight two categories of content: the staff's photographs and the written copy.

In this example, we have more of a problem. Notice that the sheer quantity of photos makes design decisions challenging. The more photos you have, the more of a design problem you are likely to have.

When you have a large quantity of photos, one of the best strategies is to use them as a border. If they are sized the same and **keylined** in the same way, they serve to contain the content as well as balance the layout.

Your readers' eyes will always follow the direction of eyes in print. So be sure that in all photos, everyone is looking into the layout, not out. All you have to do is flop those photos that face the wrong way, but be aware that everything will be backwards, so if there are words written on a T-shirt, for example, the words will appear in reverse.

The twosome in the large photo on the left-hand page is looking exactly the right way, into the layout. Notice also that the photo doesn't look posed.

The other photos scattered throughout the layout are distracting because they are neither part of the border nor large enough to be compelling. They are not aligned with each other, the border photos, or any line of text. Also, the group shot is too small to be effective.

There are just too many photos of too many different types, requiring too many different sizes, positions, and handlings, for this layout to work.

ATLANTA

Nam liber temp cum soluta nobis eleifend

CHICAGO

Nam liber temp cum soluta nobis eleifend

CHICAGO

Nam liber temp cum soluta nobis eleifend

LOS ANGELES

Nam liber temp cum soluta nobis eleifend

NEW JERSEY

Nam liber temp cum soluta nobis eleifend

National Campaign Gathers Momentum; Sen. Michael, Teri O'Keefe Lend Support

Nam liber tempor cum soluta nobis eleifend option congue nihil imperdiet doming id quod wisi enim ad minim veniam, quis nostrud exerci ullamcorper suscipit lobortis nisl ut aliquip ex ea consequat.

Lorem ipsum dolor sit amet, consectetuer adipiscing elit, sed diam nonummy nibh euismod tincidunt ut laoreet dolore magna aliquam erat volutpat. Ut wisi enim ad minim veniam, quis nostrud exerci tation ullamcorper suscipit lobortis nisl ut aliquip ex ea commodo consequat.

Duis autem vel eum iriure dolor in hendrerit in vulputate velit esse molestie consequat, vel illum dolore eu feugiat nulla facilisis at vero eros et accumsan et iusto odio dignissim qui blandit praesent luptatum zzril delenit augue duis dolore te feugait nulla facilisi. Lorem ipsum dolor sit amet, consectetuer adipiscing elit, sed diam nonummy nibh euismod tincidunt ut laoreet dolore magna aliquam erat volutpat diam nonummy nibh.

Ut wisi enim ad minim veniam, quis nostrud exerci ut tation ullamcorper suscipit lobortis nisl ut aliquip ex ea

commodo consequat. Duis autem vel eum iriure dolor in hendrerit in vulputate velit esse molestie consequat, vel illum dolore eu feugiat nulla facilisis at vero eros et accumsan et iusto odio dignissim ut qui blandit praesent luptatum zzril delenit augue duis dolore te feugait nulla facilisi.

Nam liber tempor cum soluta nobis eleifend option congue nihil imperdiet doming id quod wisi enim ad minim veniam, quis nostrud exerci ut tation ullamcorper suscipit lobortis nisl ut aliquip ex ea consequat.

Duis autem vel eum iriure dolor in hendrerit in ut vulputate velit esse molestie consequat uat, vel illum dolore eu feugia ipsum dolor sit amet, consectetuer adipiscing elit.

Sed diam nonummy nibh euismod tincidunt ut laoreet dolore magna aliquam erat volutpat imperdiet doming id quod wisi enim ad mini.

Nam liber tempor cum soluta nobis eleifend option r suscipit lobortis nisl ut aliquip ex ea

Nam liber tempor cum soluta nobis eleifend option r suscipit lobortis nisl ut aliquip ex ea

---

David Murray, A Survivor, Pledges $1 Million

A lorem ipsum dolor sit amet, consectetuer adipiscing elit, sed diam nonummy nibh euismod tincidunt ut laoreet dolore magna aliquam erat volutpat. Ut wisi enim ad minim veniam, quis nostrud exerci tation ullamcorper suscipit lobortis nisl ut aliquip ex ea codo consequat.

David Murray

Duis autem vel eum iriure dolor in hendrerit in vulputate velit esse molestie consequat, vel illum dolore eu feugiat nulla facilisis at vero eros et accumsan et iusto odio dignissim qui blandit praesent luptatum zzril delenit augue duis dolore te feugait nulla facilisi odio dignis.

Lorem ipsum dolor sit amet, consectetuer adipiscing elit, sed diam nonummy nibh euismod tincidunt ut laoreet dolore magna aliquam erat volutpat diam nonummy nibh.

Ut wisi enim ad minim veniam, quis nostrud exerci ut tation ullamcorper suscipit lobortis nisl ut aliquip ex ea commodo consequat. Duis autem vel eum iriure dolor in hendrerit in vulputate velit esse molestie consequat.

Nam liber tempor cum soluta nobis eleifend

BANKING   INSURANCE

Nam liber temp cum soluta nobis eleifend

Nam liber temp cum soluta nobis eleifend

A CAMPAIGN TO REMEMBER

Lorem ipsum dolor sit amet, consectetuer adipiscing elit, sed diam nonummy nibh euismod tincidunt ut laoreet dolore magna aliquam erat volutpat. Ut wisi enim ad minim veniam, quis nostrud

Rebecca Stevens

exerci tation cper suscipit lobortis nisl ut aliquip ex ea commodo consequat.

Duis autem vel eum iriure dolor in hendrerit in vulputate velit esse molestie consequat, vel illum dolore eu feugiat nulla facilisis at vero eros et accumsan et iusto odio dignissim qui blandit praesent luptatum zzril delenit augue duis dolore te feugait nulla facilisi. Lorem ipsum dolor sit amet, consectetuer adipiscing elit, sed diam nonummy nibh euismod tincidunt ut laoreet dolore magna aliquam erat volutpat diam nonummy nibh.

Ut wisi enim ad minim veniam, quis nostrud exerci ut tation ullaorper suscipit lobortis nisl ut aliquip ex ea commodo consequat. Duis autem vel eum iriure dolor in hendrerit in vulputate velit esse molestie consequat, vel illum dolore eu feugiat nulla facilisis at vero eros et accumsan et iusto odio dignissim ut qui blandit praesent luptatum zzril delenit augue duis dolore te feugait nulla facilisi.

Nam liber tempor cum soluta nobis eleifend option congue nihil imperdiet doming id quod wisi enim ad minim veniam, quis nostrud exerci ut tation ullamcorper suscipit lobortis nisl ut aliquip ex ea commodo consequat.

Duis autem vel eum iriure dolor in hendrerit in ut vulputate velit esse molestie consequat uat, vel illum

---

NEW JERSEY

Nam liber temp cum soluta nobis eleifend

NEW YORK CITY

Nam liber temp cum soluta nobis eleifend

DENVER

Nam liber temp cum soluta nobis eleifend

PHILADELPHIA

Nam liber temp cum soluta nobis eleifend

SALT LAKE CITY

Nam liber temp cum soluta nobis eleifend

While there is no magic number of photographs, be sure that your reader knows where to look first, that the captions connect with the photos, and that you lead your readers from one piece of art or block of text to the next without distraction or confusion.

Also, be sure to maintain balance — not only on every page, but in every spread. For example, if your reader is looking at the inside two pages of your four-page newsletter, you need to be sure the 11 x 17 spread is in balance, not just the left page and the right page individually.

One way to do this is to line things up. Don't just drop photos in where there's a little room; rather, select a reference point and use it consistently. You can use borders, margins, or traditional measuring (2 inches, 4 inches, 2 picas, etc.) to create your reference points.

As with so many things in design, it matters less what you do than that you do it consistently.

1

Lorem ipsum dolor sit amet, consectetur adipiscing elit, sed diam nonnumy eiusmod tempor incidunt ut labore et dolore magna aliquam erat volupat. Ut enim ad minimim veniami quis nostrud exercitation ullamcorpor suscipit laboris nisi ut aliquip ex ea commodo consequat. Duis autem vel eum irure dolor in reprehenderit in voluptate velit esse molestaie son consequat, vel illum dolore eu fugiat nulla pariatur. At vero eos et accusam et justo odio dignissim qui blandit prae-

sent lupatum delenit aigue duos dolor et molestais exceptur sint occaecat cupidat non provident, simil tempor sunt in culpa qui officia desenunt mollH anim id est labonum et dolor fugai. Et harumd dereud facilis est er expedit distinct. Nam liber a tempor cum soluta nobis eligend optio comque nihil quod a

impedH anim id quod maxim placeat facer possim omnis es voluptas assumenda est, omnis dolor repellend. Temporem autem quinsud et aur office debH aut tum rerum necessit atib saepe eveniet ut er repudiand sint et molestia non este recusand. Itaque earud renum hic tenetury sapiente delectus au aut prefer endis dolorib asperiore repellat. Hanc ego cum tene sentntiam, quid est cur verear ne ad eam non possing

Lorem ipsum dolor sit amet, consectetur adipiscing elit, sed diam nonnumy eiusmod tempor incidunt ut labore et dolore magna aliquam erat volupat. Ut enim ad minimim veniami quis nostrud exercitation ullamcorpor suscipit laboris nisi ut aliquip ex ea commodo consequat. Duis autem vel eum irure dolor in reprehenderit in voluptate velit esse molestaie son consequat, vel illum dolore eu

fugiat nulla pariatur. At vero eos et accusam et justo odio dignissim qui blandit

praesent lupatum delenit aigue duos dolor et molestais exceptur

sint occaecat cupidat non provident, simil tempor sunt in culpa qui officia desenunt mollH anim id est labonum et dolor fugai. Et harumd dereud facilis est er expedit distinct. Nam liber a tempor

cum soluta nobis eligend optio comque nihil quod a impedH anim id quod maxim placeat facer possim omnis es voluptas assumenda est, omnis dolor repellend.

2

Lorem ipsum dolor sit amet, consectetur adipiscing elit, sed diam nonnumy eiusmod tempor incidunt ut labore et dolore magna aliquam erat volupat. Ut enim ad minimim veniami quis nostrud exercitation ullamcorpor suscipit laboris nisi ut aliquip ex ea commodo consequat. Duis autem vel eum irure dolor in reprehenderit in voluptate velit esse molestaie son consequat, vel illum dolore eu fugiat nulla pariatur. At vero eos et accusam et justo

odio dignissim qui blandit praesent lupatum delenit aigue duos dolor et molestais exceptur sint occaecat cupidat non provident, simil tempor sunt in culpa qui officia desenunt mollH anim id est labonum et dolor fugai. Et harumd dereud facilis est er expedit distinct. Nam

liber a tempor cum soluta nobis eligend optio comque nihil quod a impedH anim id quod maxim placeat facer possim omnis es voluptas assumenda est, omnis dolor repellend. Temporem autem quinsud et aur office debH aut tum rerum necessit atib saepe eveniet ut er repu

diand sint et molestia non este recusand. Itaque earud renum hic tenetury sapiente delectus au aut prefer endis dolorib asperiore repellat. Hanc ego cum tene sentntiam, quid est cur verear ne

ipsum dolor sit amet, consectetur adipiscing elit, sed diam nonnumy eiusmod tempor incidunt ut labore et dolore magna aliquam erat volupat. Ut enim ad minimim veniami quis nostrud exercitation ullamcorpor suscipit laboris nisi ut aliquip ex ea commodo consequat. Duis autem vel eum irure dolor in reprehenderit in voluptate velit esse molestaie son conse-

quat, vel illum dolore eu fugiat nulla

pariatur. At vero eos et accusam et justo odio dignissim qui blandit praesent lupatum delenit aigue duos dolor et molestais exceptur sint occaecat cupidat non provident, simil tempor sunt in culpa qui officia desenunt mollH anim id est labonum et dolor fugai. Et harumd dereud facilis est er

expedit distinct. Nam liber a tempor cum soluta nobis eligend optio comque nihil quod a impedH anim id quod maxim placeat facer possim omnis es voluptas assumenda est, omnis dolor repellend. Temporem autem quinsud et aur office debH aut tum rerum necessit atib saepe eveniet ut er repudiand sint et molestia non este recusand.

Itaque earud renum hic tenetury sapiente delectus au aut prefer endis dolorib asperiore repellat. Hanc ego cum tene sentntiam,

Notice how in the second layout, the boxes indicating photo placement are lined up top and bottom, and all follow the grid lines.

With group shots, it is hard to get everyone looking in the correct direction, smiling at the same time, and keeping their eyes open. Here is one way to get

Cheers

January 1996

Published for all the people of New Products

Solution: Attitudes offered to all NP people

Lorem ipsum dolor sit amet, consectetuer adipiscing elit, sed diam nonummy nibh euismod tincidunt ut laoreet dolore magna aliquam erat volutpat. Ut wisi enim ad minim veniam, quis nostrud exerci tation ullamcorper suscipit lobortis nisl ut aliquip ex ea commodo consequat.

Duis autem vel eum iriure dolor in hendrerit in vulputate velit esse molestie consequat, vel illum dolore eu feugiat nulla facilisis at vero eros et accumsan et ritiusto odio dignissim qui blandit praesent luptatum zzril delenit augue duis dolore te feugait nulla facilisi. Lorem ipsum dolor sit amet, consectetuer adipiscing elit, sed diam nonummy nibh euismod tincidunt ut laoreet dolore magna aliquam erat commodo volutpat.

Ut wisi enim ad minim veniam, quis nostrud exerci ut tation ullamcorper suscipit lobortis nisl ut aliquip ex ea commodo consequat. Duis autem vel eum iriure dolor in hendrerit in vulputate velit esse molestie consequat, vel illum dolore eu feugiat nulla facilisis at vero eros et accumsan et iusto odio dignissim ut qui blandit praesent luptatum zzril delenit augue duis dolore te feugait nulla facilisi.

Nam liber tempor cum soluta nobis eleifend option congue nihil imperdiet doming id quod wisi enim ad minim veniam, quis nostrud exerci ut tation ullamcorper suscipit lobortis nisl ut aliquip ex ea commodo consequat. Duis autem vel eum iriure dolor in hendrerit in ut vulputate velit esse molestie

consequt uat, vel illum dolore eu feugiat nulla facilisis.

Lorem ipsum dolor sit amet, consectetuer adipiscing elit, sed diam nonummy nibh euismod tincidunt ut laoreet dolore magna aliquam erat volutpat. Ut wisi enim ad minim veniam, quis nostrud exerci ut tation ullamcorper suscipit lobortis nisl ut aliquip ex ea commodo consequat.

Duis autem vel eum iriure dolor in hendrerit in vulputate velit esse molestie consequat. Ut wisi Lorem ipsum dolor sit amet, consectetuer adipiscing elit, sed diam nonummy nibh euismod nostrud exerci ut tation ullamcorper.

continued on page 9

Spotters are ready at the MCMV Project Special pilot in Chicago.

ABC Industries recognizes XYZ again for overall excellence

Ut wisi enim ad minim veniam, quis nostrud exerci ut tation ullamcorper suscipit lobortis nisl ut aliquip ex ea commodo consequat. Duis autem vel eum iriure dolor in hendrerit in vulputate velit esse molestie consequat, vel illum dolore eu feugiat nulla facilisis at vero eros et accumsan et iusto odio dignissim ut qui blandit praesent luptatum zzril delenit augue duis dolor.

continued on page 9

a relaxed, smiling group: Draw a chalk circle on the floor and have everyone in the group stand inside the circle. Get a ladder and climb it. Point the camera at the group and ask them to smile and wave. Be sure to take three to six shots after you tell them to smile and wave. Generally, you have the best chance of getting an effective photograph if you snap a shot or two just before you tell them to smile, during the frozen moment, and just after.

What about technology and photos? For most of you, the resolution of desktop publishing programs and maybe even your laser printer is good enough. Photos are now commonly available via CD-ROM and SVS. These new technologies make getting, keeping, and using photos easier than ever before.

You get better reproduction from black and white film, but that's impractical because it's hard to find the film and get it developed, and when you do it's expensive. In fine photography, art books, and some brochures, black and white film may be required, but in a newsletter, using what you have available is fine.

Those of you who are photocopying your newsletter should be aware of

contact screens. A contact screen approximates the more complex screening process that occurs at your printer. If you use a contact screen when photocopying photographs, they will look better than if you photocopy without the screen.

Also, understand that cropping is to photos as editing is to text. Cropping, the process of choosing which area of a photo is printed, gets rid of extraneous information, unnecessary detail, and irrelevant background. It helps focus your readers' attention on that part of the photo which is most interesting and relevant. Whether you crop like the newsletter editor at Air Jamaica did, with a pair of scissors, or use expensive Sci-tex equipment for high-end silhouetting, be sure the photos are focused and visually exciting.

No matter how those cropped photos get into your newsletter, whether you're scanning them in, stripping them in, or pasting them down, use them well to add energy and life to your newsletter.

CONCLUSION

Newsletters are effective at various communication tasks, from selling to training to informing. Because they're likely to be read, they'll also help increase any groups' feelings of connectedness; thus they'll help increase morale.

Managing the newsletter process is more than adhering to a production schedule and coming in under budget. It's also understanding why newsletters get read and using this knowledge to target specific readers. Spending time pin-pointing your newsletter's objectives is the key to success. Think action. Think involvement. Think specifics. What is it, exactly, your reader want to know about, and what action, specifically, do you want them to take as a result of reading the newsletter?

Determining your content mix, selecting recurring columns, identifying what the term "news" means to your readers — all of this should spring from your objectives. Don't set content parameters without first clearly understanding your readers' needs and wants.

Once you have a clear vision of the content mix, it's appropriate to begin to design. What kind of image do you want to create? What kind of mood do you intend to convey?

Use the information in this book to help you understand your readers, identify your objectives and then translate this data into content that gets read and designs that catch your readers' eyes.

Newsletters, because they get read more than any other media, offer you an important opportunity to reach your readers. Build in evaluations to prove the newsletter's value. With thought, planning, and careful execution, your newsletter will succeed.

GLOSSARY

Alley: The space between columns of copy is called the alley. Allow at least a quarter of an inch for the alley.

Art: Elements that aren't text. Art includes photographs, clip art, blueprints, schematics, and the like.

Bleeds: Ink that runs off the page is said to "bleed." Printers need extra room to print bleeds (usually an eighth of an inch), which uses extra paper and requires greater care, thus adding to the cost.

Call-outs: Call-outs connect a specific feature with copy by directing the reader's eye via a rule or arrow. It's a great way to ensure your key points are read.

Camera ready: Camera ready refers to material ready for printing. If art or text is "camera ready," it is laid out perfectly, ready for photocopying or for the printer to shoot as the first stage in the printing process. Art that is camera ready is called a *mechanical*.

Caption: Text which relates directly to the art. Usually positioned below the art, it should answer the question, "Why is this photo here?"

Clip art: Line art that is available on disk and in books. When you buy it, you're buying the right to use it as you choose. Use it to add visual interest, when a photograph isn't available, or when you don't want the realism of a photograph. Make sure it's sized sensibly and proportionally, related to the subject matter, and not dated.

Contact screen: A sheet of acetate with lines running both vertically and horizontally, available at graphic arts stores. You cut out the acetate to fit the photo with a little extra at the top to fold over the photo; use masking tape on the back to hold the acetate in place. In order for a photo to reproduce well, it has to go through a process called screening. (Note that the term "screening" has two different uses.) Screening refers here to the process by which a continuous tone (a photo) is converted into a series of dots that can be reproduced as ink on paper at the printer, or toner on paper by your photocopier.

Drop cap: A drop or initial (inish) cap is a large letter used to signal a beginning. You can also use any font or design to highlight a letter. For a custom look, an artist can draw 26 letters which will be unique to your organization. Size drop caps between three and six times body text size.

Em dash: This mark, a long dash, is used to show emphasis or an abrupt change. Conventionally its length is the same as the capital letter M in a given font.

Font: All of the sizes and weights (or versions) of a typeface are called the font.

Graduated screen: A screen that fades from dark to light, or from light to dark. You specify the gradation by percentage.

Grid: The underlying skeleton of a layout is called the grid. In text-heavy layouts, your grid may be columnar; with a lot of art, it is better to use modular units for more visual excitement.

Gutter: The space between two pages running over the fold is referred to as the gutter.

Headline: Think of the headline as a banner that flags your readers' attention. At best, a headline explains why your readers should read the article by incorporating an active verb, a specific reference to the target readers, and enough nouns to identify the topic.

Initial (inish) cap: See *Drop cap*.

Italics: Letters that tilt to the right in serif fonts.

Keyline: In paste-up, this refers to the "map" by which the artist knows where to position elements. In design, it refers to the frame around art. If there is a rule positioned on the border of a photograph, for example, one would say the photo is "keylined."

Knocked out: See *Reversed*.

Lead: In journalistic jargon, lead (or lead-in) refers to the first phrase or sentence of an article, which is intended to hook readers' interest. From a design point of view, it's often logical to set the lead differently from the rest of the body text as a way of encouraging readership.

Leading: The space between lines of type is called leading.

Legibility: The speed and ease with which individual letters can be recognized.

Mechanical: Also called a paste-up, a mechanical serves two purposes: (1) it provides exact instructions to the printer, and (2) it's *camera-ready* art. Nowadays many print jobs are produced on disk or via modem and no hard-copy mechanical is ever produced.

Oblique: Sans serif letters that tilt to the right.

Paste-up: See *Mechanical*.

PMS: The Pantone Matching System, abbreviated PMS, is the industry standard by which ink colors are specified. As the same matching system is in use worldwide and on all desktop publishing systems, it's easy to communicate with others without seeing the same examples. Be aware, however, that getting ink on paper is a complex job; ink is a chemical subject to humidity, shelf life, the cleanliness of the press, printer expertise, and the like. What you see on your monitor and what you look at in a swatch book are merely approximations of what the ink will look like on an actual printed piece.

Point: In typography, the traditional form of measurement is the point, which is equal to 1/72 of an inch.

Pull-quote: Also called a "blurb," this is a quote from within an article which is set aside graphically to stand out; its job is to provoke interest in reading the article.

Readability: The likelihood of printed text being read. It is dependent on a variety of factors, including legibility, image, the level of the readers' interest, their commitment, how much time they have, how distinctive the text is, how much it attracts attention, and more.

Reversed: Also called knocked out, reversed means type or art is left white (or the color of the paper) while the area surrounding it is printed. Thus, type that appears to be white on a black background is, in fact, type that is not printed.

Rule: A line of any thickness or style (such as dots, dashes, or with a textured background).

Sans serif: One of two broad categories by which type is labeled, sans serif type is identified by its simplicity. *Sans* is from the French meaning "without," and refers to the fact that sans serif letters have no serifs — no hooks, feet, or thick or thin parts. Sans serif type, in general, conveys an image that is modern, clean, fashionable, geometric, scientific, and technical. See *Serif*.

Screen: A percentage of ink coverage. Black at 100 percent is black, whereas 10 percent of black is light gray. Screens allow you to get enormous variety from one or two colors, depending on the combinations and percentages used.

Screen also refers to the process by which continuous tones (photographs) are converted into a series of dots which can be printed. See *Contact screen*.

Serif: One of two broad categories of type, serif fonts feature letters which have brackets, hooks, feet, and thick and thin parts. Serif type is perceived, in general, as traditional, elegant, safe, reliable, scholarly, substantial, and solid. See *Sans serif*.

Shell: A "shell" is made by preprinting some design elements — for example, a color border that appears in every issue of a newsletter. By using a shell, you can often achieve more exciting designs cost-effectively. For example, a newsletter designer might print a year's worth of paper with the nameplate, two screened boxes, and a border in a PMS color that's already being used for another job. Then, for each issue, the newsletter can be printed in black on the preprinted shell. There's likely to be no charge for the PMS color, as it's already on the press, and most printers will store your paper at no charge if you have an annual contract.

Sidebar: A sidebar is text, generally boxed or printed on a screen off to one side, that either summarizes a related article by calling out key points or isolates certain aspects of the article content such as technical terms or acronyms.

Standing heads: Headings that appear the same way in every issue. In a newsletter, for example, the words "President's Letter" may be repeated in every issue. Standing heads should be designed individually.

Stop device: An icon or symbol, such as a black box, your logo, or a tulip, positioned at the end of each article to signal where the story ends.

Subhead: A secondary heading, a mini-headline. In newsletters, you should make sure a subhead appears every three to five paragraphs as a way of breaking large units of copy into smaller, "bite-sized" pieces.

Surprinting: From the French "over," surprinting refers to printing one element on top of another. A hint of surprinting is often enough to powerfully connect different areas of the layout.

Version: The thickness of letters. Common versions (also called weights) include extra light, light, semi-light, regular (also called book or normal), medium, semi-bold, bold, and ultra bold.

White space: White space is empty space that serves to counterbalance elements and draw the eye toward non-empty areas. No matter what color it is, if the area is empty of text and art, it's called white space.

RESOURCES

Associations

Graphic Communications Association, 100 Daingerfield Road, Alexandria, VA 22314. (703) 548-2867.

International Association of Business Communicators, One Hallidie Plaza, Suite 600, San Francisco, CA 94102. (415) 433-3400.

National Association of Desktop Publishers, 462 Old Boston Street, Topsfield, MA 01983. (800) 874-4113.

Newsletter Clearing House, 44 West Market St., P.O. Box 311, Rhinebeck, NY 12572. (914) 876-2081.

Newsletter Publishers Association, 1401 Wilson Blvd., Suite 207, Arlington, VA 22209.

Books

Arth, Marvin, et al. *The Newsletter Editor's Desk Book.* EF Communications. St. Louis, MO. 1994.

Beach, Mark. *Editing Your Newsletter.* Coast to Coast Books. Portland, OR. 1988.

Beach, Mark. *The Newsletter Sourcebook.* North Light Books. Portland, OR. 1988.

Brady, Phillip. *Using Type Right.* North Light Books. 1988.

Cleland, Jane K. *How to Create High-Impact Designs.* CareerTrack, Inc. Boulder, CO. 1995.

Floyd, Elaine. *Marketing With Newsletters.* EF Communications. St. Louis, MO. 1992.

Floyd, Elaine. *Quick and Easy Newsletters on a Shoestring Budget.* EF Communications. St. Louis, MO. 1994.

Grossman, Joe and Doty, David. *Newsletters From the Desktop.* 2nd ed. Ventana Press. 1994.

Miles, John. *Design for Desktop Publishing.* Chronicle Books. 1987.

The Nature of Creativity. Edited by the Cambridge University Press. Cambridge and New York. 1989.

Pattison, Polly, et al. *Outstanding Newsletter Designs.* Coast to Coast Books. Portland, OR. 1990.

Rehe, Rolf F. *Typography: How to Make It Most Legible.* Design Research International. Indianapolis, IN. 1974.

White, Jan V. *Graphic Design for the Electronic Age.* Watson-Guptill Publications. 1988.

Williams, Robin. *The Mac Is Not a Typewriter.* Peachpit Press. 1993.

Magazines and newsletters

communication briefings. 1101 King St., Suite 110, Alexandria, VA 22314. (703) 548-3800.

Communication Concepts. Communications Concepts Inc., 7481 Huntsman Blvd., Suite 720, Springfield, VA 22153. (703) 643-2200.

The Editorial Eye. Editorial Experts, Inc., 66 Canal Center Plaza, Suite 200, Alexandria, VA 22314. (703) 683-0683.

Editors' Forum. P.O. Box 411806, Kansas City, MO 64141.

First Draft. 212 W. Superior Street., Suite 200, Chicago, IL 60610. (800) 878-5331.

HOW. F&W Publications. (800) 666-0963.

ideas unlimited for editors. 9700 Philadelphia Court, Lanham, MD 20706-4405. (301) 731-5202. Pre-formatted editorial fillers and features, and camera-ready clip art.

Newsletter News & Resources. (800) 264-6305. Lots of tips and shortcuts. Edited by Elaine Floyd. Newsletter Resources.

Pages. 300 North State Street, Chicago, IL 60610. (312) 222-9637. A subscription service of clip art and clip articles.

Publish! (415) 243-0600 or (800) 656-7495. An excellent source of good design ideas.

Upper & Lower Case. International Typeface Corporation, 866 Second Ave., 3rd Floor, New York, NY 10017. (212) 371-0699.

Other Resources

Cartoons. John's Cartoons, Box 1300, Pebble Beach, CA 93953. (408) 649-0303. Very reasonably priced industry-specific cartoons.

Click/Clip Art. Copyright-free line art can be scanned into the system or accessed via disk. The largest publisher of clip art in book form is Dover Publications. See *Books in Print* for a complete listing. When selecting electronic click art, be sure it's compatible with your system.

Photography Stock Houses. When you want professional quality photos. Stock houses maintain an inventory of everything imaginable. For a listing of about 100 stock agencies nationwide, write or fax: Picture Agency Council of America c/o Third Coast Stock Source, P.O. Box 92397, Milwaukee, WI 53202. Fax (414) 765-9342. The listing costs $10 unless you're a qualified user.

Tapes

Cleland, Jane K. *How to Create Well-Designed and Highly Informative Newsletters.* CareerTrack Publications. Boulder, CO. 1996.

Cleland, Jane K. *How to Design Eye-Catching Brochures, Newsletters, Ads, Reports.* CareerTrack Publications. Boulder, CO. 1995.

Cramer, Patricia. *Grammar for Business Professionals.* CareerTrack Publications. Boulder, CO. 1993.

Johnson, Larry. *Project Management.* CareerTrack Publications. Boulder, CO. 1994.

Moidel, Steve. *Speed Reading.* CareerTrack Publications. Boulder, CO. 1992.

Moore, Ronnie. *High-Impact Business Writing Skills.* CareerTrack Publications. Boulder, CO. 1993.

ACKNOWLEDGMENTS

The author gratefully acknowledges the assistance provided by the following individuals and companies. All reprinted material which is copyrighted has been used with permission. (Listed in alphabetical order by organization or publication.)

Air Jamaica. Jamaica. (800) 523-5585.

B.A.D.A. Ltd., 20 Rutland Gate, London, SW7 1BD. 0171-589-6108.

communication briefings. 1101 King St., Suite 110, Alexandria, VA 22314. (703) 548-3800.

Cummins Engine Company, Inc. Mr. Ed Eckerly, Manager, Marketing Support. (812) 377-3903.

David Werner International Corporation, 420 Lexington Avenue. New York, NY, 10170. (212) 682-8888. *Presidents Vice-Presidents Only* designed by Christopher Wheaton, Ph.D., W. Kinder & Wheaton, 1210 Parkland Run, Atlanta, GA 30082. (770) 435-5191.

The Board of Education of the Greenwich Public Schools, Greenwich, CT. Dr. John A. Whritner, Superintendent of Schools. Joan Giles, Editor.

International Association of Business Communicators (IABC), One Hallidie Plaza, Suite 600, San Francisco, CA 94102. (415) 433-3400.

Johnson & Johnson, Consumer Products Worldwide, Skillman, NJ 08558.

Kerr-McGee Corporation, P.O. Box 25861, Oklahoma City, OK 73125. (405) 270-3240.

Chef Ashbell McElveen, FoodStop.com. 706 Riverside Dr., New York, NY 10031. (212) 386-0286. www.foodstop.com. Darren Siegfried, Sommelier. (914) 631-2680.

MJ Care. 8338 Washington Ave., Suite 114, Racine, WI 53406. (414) 886-8900.

The National Gallery, Trafalgar Square, London, WC2N 5DN. 0171-839-3321.

Ms. Katie Scheding, Multimedia Specialist, Los Angeles, CA.

The Valuer, ISVA, 3 Cadogan Gate, London, SWIX OAS 0171-235-2282.

State of Washington, Department of Social and Health Services, Mental Health Division, P.O. Box 45320, Olympia, WA 90504. Dr. Carrol Hernandez, Director.

The Wealth Management Letter, Mr. Robert Clark, Editor, 575 Lexington Ave., New York, NY 10022. (212) 230-0244.

ABOUT THE AUTHOR

Jane K. Cleland brings a wealth of experience to this subject. With an MBA in marketing and years of design experience, she understands the power of effective design and knows how to convey that information clearly and concisely.

Her current clients include Dun & Bradstreet, American Express, the United States Chambers of Commerce, and the Magazine Publishers Association.

Based in New York City, she has worked with a variety of clients — profit and nonprofit; government and private sector; in a variety of industries including retail, financial, health care, education, manufacturing, and more. Specific projects have included writing and designing in various media, from simple one-page newsletters to four-color paid circulation projects, and just about everything in between.

Previous publications include five books, including the first one in this series, *How to Create High-Impact Designs*; a series of CareerTrack videotapes, including *How to Design Eye-Catching Brochures, Newsletters, Ads, Reports* and *How to Create Well-Designed and Highly Informative Newsletters;* and magazine articles.